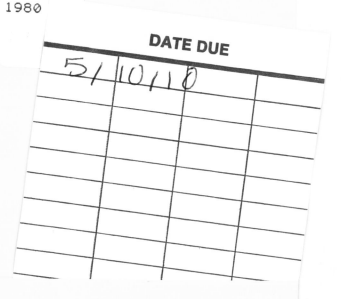

DATE DUE

5/10/10

The Bargain

The Bargain

The Story behind the 30-Year Honeymoon of GM and the UAW

Kathy Groehn El-Messidi

NELLEN PUBLISHING COMPANY INC.
NEW YORK

Designed and Produced by The Bookmakers, Incorporated/
John Beck and Jim Bernard

Library of Congress Cataloging in Publication Data

El-Messidi, Kathy Groehn, 1946–
   The bargain.

   Includes index.
   1. Collective bargaining—Automobile industry—United
States—History—Case studies. 2. International Union,
United Automobile, Aerospace, and Agricultural Implement
Workers of America. 3. General Motors Corporation.
I. Title.
HD6976.A82U55   331.89′042′920973   78-26325
ISBN 0-8424-0120-2

To Dad
whose enthusiasm for his work
enriched our lives

Contents

Preface

From a table of scrambled demands, counterproposals and stalemates, the largest industrial union and the richest company in the United States grabbed and bought The Bargain one spring day in 1948. As postwar prosperity dawned, it seemed to the United Auto Workers and General Motors that the best price was obtained for industrial peace and the lowest cost for inflation. Both parties pieced together, then adopted, a bold and unique combination of wage escalation, productivity factoring and long-term bargaining.

Wage escalation meant workers gained automatic increases or decreases in their wages as living costs rose or fell. This was dependent upon changes in the Consumer Price Index (CPI), a measure of the workers' "market basket" which is a standardized set of typical purchases monitored by the United States Bureau of Labor Statistics (BLS).

Productivity factoring recognized that workers deserved regular percentage wage increases because they added to America's ability to produce more goods with the same amount of effort. Such increases rested on historical average yearly increases in output per man hour for

United States manufacturing industries, regardless of cost of living changes.

Because workers' incomes kept up with their living costs and they received dependable wage increases, General Motors officials anticipated fewer strikes and negotiations. The contract would then last two years instead of one, and they could look forward to even longer lasting future contracts.

Acknowledgments

Several helping hands and research centers facilitated this study. George B. Morris, Jr., GM's Vice President, Industrial Relations Staff, and Anthony DeLorenzo, GM's Vice President, Public Relations Staff, arranged for my access to helpful material at the General Motors Building in Detroit. Clifford Merriott, GM News Relations Director, Jim Crellin of the GM News Relations Staff and William Brunstad, GM's Assistant Director of Labor Relations, discussed the 1948 contract implications with me. The Public Relations library staff at the GM building helped me locate pertinent books, magazine articles, biographies and speeches. Their 45-volume collection of published comments, *Wage Escalator and Inflationary Spiral,* encompassing 1948 to the present time, proved a thorough source.

Joan Spring, Senior Statistician at GM's Economic Relations Library, located pertinent research and publications of company, government, union and independent organizations.

General Motors officials gave me access to certain vital but confidential information concerning the 1948 GM-UAW negotiations. My access to this material was restricted to and solely for my use as background information. It was made available so that my interviews with participants in the negotiations would be more meaningful. I am not permitted to quote from these documents or describe the nature of them. Much of what they contained was fortunately corroborated by participants in the negotiations and was reported herein to the extent they were willing to permit attribution.

The Jack W. Skeels oral history, housed at Walter Reuther Labor Archives, Detroit, Michigan, detailed UAW and Communist Party activities prior to the settlement. It amply developed Reuther's rise to power, so crucial to the topic's background. Warner Pflug, Dr. Philip Mason and Di Miles at the archives acquainted me with their material and arranged crucial interviews with United Automobile Workers and Communist Party figures. Elizabeth Haarz Petersen, my cousin, helped me pick up the pace and depth of my research there. Tom Kleene of the *Detroit Free Press* and Jack Crellin of the *Detroit News*, two seasoned automotive and labor reporters, gave me their unique insights and special assistance, and I thank them.

The Charles Erwin Wilson Archives at Anderson, Indiana held disappointingly little information on Wilson's development of and involvement with the concepts. However, its records contained insights into his lifestyle and corporate life. Lynn Goldman helped me use this collection.

This study is a revision of my doctoral dissertation, completed under the advisory and professional eye of Dr. H. Wayne Morgan at the University of Oklahoma. Dr. Morgan generously shared the knowledge he obtained from editing and authoring fifteen of his own works. Also helpful was the support given me by other author-professors on my dissertation committee: Dr. David Levy, Dr. Arrell M. Gibson, and Dr. Norman Crockett.

In a more personal vein, I am grateful to my husband, Adel, and my mother, Mrs. Thomas Groehn, for their continual confidence in me. I would never have undertaken this work without the interst of my father, the late Thomas Groehn, a former news relations director for General Motors, who encouraged me in my writing and educational career. Finally, I would not have completed this study without the support of Carolyn Swan of Oklahoma City, Oklahoma.

Introducing the Participants

LABOR

Addes, George	United Automobile Workers Union secretary-treasurer, 1936-1947.
Anderson, John	United Automobile Workers Union executive board member, 1936-1937; Local 15 president, 1946-1949; proffered wage-escalation proposals in conventions of 1947 preceding 1948 adoption of escalation.
Conway, Jack	United Automobile Workers Union negotiating team member, 1948.
Frankensteen, Richard	United Automobile Workers Union member who was a latecomer in joining the Addes-Thomas-Reuther Unity Caucus opposing Homer Martin. Accompanied Walter Reuther and was beaten in the Battle of the Overpass at the Ford plant in 1937.
Green, William	American Federation of Labor president who, with Charles Erwin Wilson of General Motors, recommended a 45-hour work week to remedy post–World War II inflation.

Hoffa, James R.	Teamster president who by late 1940's and early 1950's vied for Michigan political power among Democrats.
Johnstone, Thomas Arthur	Director of General Motors Department of UAW and negotiator in 1948; later, head of Labor Relations for Canadian National Railway.
Lewis, John L.	United Mine Worker president and Congress of Industrial Organizations President who sided with George Addes opposing Franklin D. Roosevelt and Walter Reuther on entering more actively in World War II in 1939.
Livingston, Jack	United Automobile Workers president and a chief negotiator in 1948.
Martin, Homer	United Automobile Workers president in earliest organizing years of the union; defeated in struggle for union control by the Unity Caucus, made up of Addes, Thomas, Reuther and others. Martin was supported by the AFL as the Unity Caucus won the support of the CIO, 1938-1939.
Mazey, Emil	United Automobile Workers executive board member who in 1946 was in Walter Reuther's camp when Reuther was a United Automobile Workers president with a minority of executive board support; he served as UAW Secretary Treasurer for many years under Reuther and his successors.
Michener, Lew	United Automobile Workers executive board member who led aircraft wildcat strikes opposed by Walter Reuther but supported by George Addes at center of 1941 power controversy.

Murray, Philip	President of the CIO from November 1940 through 1952.
Palmer, Jack	President of United Automobile Workers Union, Local 659, and leader of the "Five Presidents" Movement that sought to include wage escalation and other demands in the 1948 United Automobile Workers Union platform. Walter Reuther quieted their vigorous and well-supported campaign in 1948, just before negotiations got under way.
Reuther, Victor	United Automobile Workers Education Department director, 1947. Brother of Walter Reuther.
Reuther, Walter	United Automobile Workers president, 1947-1970.
Stellato, Carl	Walter Reuther's enemy from Ford Local 600, the UAW's largest local, who challenged the UAW president in 1952, seeking shorter-term contracts. He lost.
Thomas, R.J.	United Automobile Workers president, 1939-1946. His appointment of and support of Walter Reuther as director of the vital General Motors Department of the United Automobile Workers proved to be crucial. Reuther was vice president to Thomas in 1941; Thomas became Reuther's Vice President in 1947.
Weinberg, Nathan	United Automobile Workers research director who compiled and presented statistics during the 1948 negotiations, when statistics became more important than ever before.

INDUSTRY

Breech, Ernest	Former General Motors executive hired by Henry Ford II in 1945 to

	correct faults in postwar Ford management.
Court, Andrew	Member of General Motors business research staff who in 1941 helped Charles E. Wilson formulate General Motor's concepts for the 1948 contract.
DuBrul, Stephen	Director of General Motors business research staff; former director of Social and Economic Relations within General Motors personnel staff, 1946; helped Charles E. Wilson formulate the 1948 contract concepts in 1941.
Ford, Henry Ford II	Grandson of Henry Ford I who became Ford Motor Company president in 1945, and tried to improve its management.
Knudsen, William	General Motors president, 1937-1940.
Morris, George B., Jr.	General Motors labor-relations staff member in 1948 who, as vice president of labor relations in the 1970's judged that The Bargain helped General Motors labor-management relations considerably.
Rising, Frank	Automotive Parts Association president who publicly challenged Wilson on his introduction of escalation.
Seaton, Louis	Appointed General Motors director of labor relations in 1946; a major negotiator in 1948 in that position; later became vice president in charge of personnel.
Sloan, Alfred P., Jr.	General Motors president, 1923-1937. As early as 1934, he considered the possibility of adjusting GM's wages to cost-of-living increases.

Wilson, Charles Erwin

General Motors president, 1941-1953; credited with the development of specific cost-of-living adjustment and productivity adjustment proposals offered in the 1948 negotiations.

GOVERNMENT

Blankenhorn, Heber

National Labor Relations Board member who resigned because he believed the Taft-Hartley Act harmed labor organization.

Clague, Ewan

Commissioner of Labor Statistics, Bureau of Labor Statistics, 1946-1954.

Lubin, Isadore

Commissioner of Labor Statistics, 1933-46.

Taft, Robert

Ohio senator since 1938; in 1948, he ran as the Republican presidential candidate against incumbent President Truman and lost; he coauthored the Taft-Hartley Act of 1947.

Truman, Harry S

U.S. president, 1945-1952; he struggled uncertainly with the problem of inflation in the post–World War II period.

Wallace, Henry Agard

Secretary of Agriculture, 1933-40; vice-president under Franklin Roosevelt, 1941-45; in 1948 his political leanings became "progressive," more to the left of President Truman, and he led a short-lived Progressive party ticket.

OTHERS

Brams, Stanley

Representative of McGraw-Hill publications in Detroit; edited and published *Detroit Labor Trends*.

Crellin, Jack

Labor reporter, *Detroit News*.

Ganley, Nat

Daily Worker columnist who downgraded the 1948 settlement when it was announced.

Harbison, Frederick

University of Chicago researcher who judged that The Bargain would stabilize collective bargaining in mass-production industries.

Kleene, Tom

Detroit Free Press general business writer; worked on *Detroit News, Detroit Times* and *Detroit Free Press* at various times since 1936.

Jordan, Virgil

National Industrial Conference Board director whose letter to Alfred Sloan indicated that cost-of-living wage-adjustment formulas would probably be unacceptable to labor and General Motors; advocated cost-of-living figures as an underlying measure for wage adjustment, April 1941.

Soffer, Benson

Scholarly researcher who found that The Bargain sustained real wages during inflation, but shortchanged wage increases during more stable price periods, 1954.

Taylor, Frederick

"Scientific Management" engineer of the late nineteenth and early twentieth centuries who thought cost-of-living wage adjustment would prevent union organization.

Trotsky, Leon

Bolshevik leader second in power to Lenin until his death in 1924; lost to Stalin in power struggle which followed, and was expelled from the Communist party in 1927; from his exile in Mexico in 1938, he formulated ideas about the use of wage and hour "sliding scales" in order to forward the socialist revolution. Murdered in 1940.

THOSE WHO WITNESSED SIGNING OF CONTRACT
AND ARE LISTED IN A PAMPHLET ENTITLED
"AGREEMENT BETWEEN GENERAL MOTORS CORPO-
RATION AND THE UAW-CIO," MAY 29, 1948.
INTERNATIONAL UNION,
UNITED AUTOMOBILE,
AIRCRAFT AND AGRICULTURAL
IMPLEMENT WORKERS OF
AMERICA, CIO

(S)   John W. Livingston
        Thomas A. Johnstone
        Joseph J. Zingaro
        Daniel J. Odneal
        Ralph L. Smith
        Glenn A. Rexford
        Henry H. Weston
        John Fairbairn
        Elmer Yenney
        Walter S. Park
        Charles K. Beckman
        Jack T. Conway
        E.S. Patterson

GENERAL MOTORS
CORPORATION

(S)   H.W. Anderson
        Louis G. Seaton
        H.T. Gierok
        E.R. Bramblett
        F.H. Schwarze
        H.D. Garrett
        G.L. Wright
        G.B. Morris, Jr.

1

Postwar America
Renewal and Uncertainty

In the spring of 1948, United Automobile Worker president Walter Reuther had just become secure in his hard-won power when an assailant sneaked up to a rear window of his home, shot him, and escaped, never to be apprehended.

The man who brought new, unified strength to the UAW entrusted negotiations to his staff as he tried to recover use of his damaged right arm. They consulted him sparingly in the hospital and at home. Without his approval, an agreement would certainly founder.

Charles Erwin Wilson had also been hospitalized when he first attained General Motors' presidency in 1941. He had used his idle hospital hours to prepare new ideas for labor relations, which he readied for the 1948 negotiations. During this session, his labor relations staff took frequent elevator trips to his upstairs office in the General Motors Building for consultation. Vital offstage cues were whispered to negotiators, who, like actors, would not let the press or the government hear any news until they were certain of their lines. This surprised both reporters and federal mediators.

Consequently, Americans, whom The Bargain would greatly touch, knew little about it until it became fact. Peacetime institutions developed so that public intervention in labor relations was nearly impossible. No influential consumer advocates spoke for the people. They spoke for themselves at the ballot box and at the cash register. If they harbored doubts about The Bargain, they might refuse to buy. But in 1948, they craved cars. Prosperity reaffirmed capitalism regardless of the latter's theoretical or ideological deviations.

Everyone assumed that capitalism no longer operated (if it ever had) under perfect competitive market situations: many competing firms regulated by an "invisible hand." Large companies which made significant consumer goods won out, estimated their market shares well, knew their competition and priced through informal agreements or wise guesses. Most postwar Americans accepted industrial concentration, or assumed that Attorney General Thurman Arnold's antitrust suits would remove bad trusts. They appreciated big-business efficiency and sensed this was a poor time to break up companies. They assumed corporations competed through new improved products, advertising and salesmanship.

Few asked why "The New Duz is the finest Duz that Ever Wuz," but the slogan conveyed the sense of postwar renewal and record prosperity. The once "sovereign consumer" fell prey to advertising and salesmanship, and was not always able to evaluate new experimental products well. There were mattresses with heating units; magnetized kitchen tools that mixed drinks and scoured pots; and hangar-house communities, where private pilots flew onto community runways, then taxied into hangars attached to their houses. There was a peculiar picture box called television. For the public, foam fought fires and mechanical hands manipulated radioactive materials.

Consumers revelled in new goods and largely overlooked the structure of capitalism. They bought more department store and catalog goods than ever before. Americans probably smirked at stories that the manager of Moscow's largest department store received overpriced, defective stocks of shoes from Russian factories. The same manager worried that potato peeling machines which were in high demand could be made, but were not, and that Russians did not manufacture bookshelves or window screens.

American workers got better pay but worked fewer hours than before. An average industrial worker received about double his prewar wage, $1.25 an hour in 1947. The country earned a record two hundred billion dollars with which it could almost buy back the unprecedented two hundred thirty-five billion dollars worth of goods and services it produced. Only about 3 percent of the United States work force remained idle. Corporations received seventeen billion dollars after taxes, and farmers, eighteen billion. The country exported more than it had in the most active World War II year.

New Deal and wartime programs levelled the populace into a larger middle class. Average Americans jingled more money in their pockets than ever before. Withdrawals exceeded savings by one billion dollars in 1947, but blue collar workers earned and saved more than white collar workers during and after World War II.

The vice president of a Pittsburgh Planned Parenthood Clinic had triplets in 1948, as the United States birthrate that normally hovered around 17.5 births per thousand escalated to 25 per thousand. Wartime marriages and babies spurred the boom, but a postwar desire for family life maintained the initiative. Production seemed to keep up with population increases, so that living standards might either stabilize or improve.

The government recorded over one-and-a-half billion dollars in surplus, and expected it to rise to six or seven billion dollars after tax collection in June. President Truman felt expansive enough to build a back porch on the White House for fifteen thousand dollars which architects deplored and Truman defended as "outside breathing space" away from public view. In Hollywood, Ann Blyth bested the president when she got a custom-fitted eigh-teen-thousand-dollar mermaid tail to wear in a 1948 movie spectacular. Walt Disney, too, got richer than ever—thanks to *Bambi*.

Americans gave more money than ever before to churches, and community chests and charities set record goals for their drives. People around the world received more than twenty thousand CARE packages daily from the United States. The two-and-a-half billion dollars citizens gave to charity paled in comparison to what they spent on beer and liquor ($8.7 billion), horse-betting ($6 billion), and tobacco ($3.4 billion). Charitable contributions represented only 2 percent of their incomes compared with the 5 per-cent depression-ridden Americans gave.

Abundance could not erase the twelve-year shadows of depression and war. Many worried about recession re-curring, as it had eighteen months after World War I in the 1920 downturn. One commentator concluded that re-cession did strike again, eighteen months after World War II, but the country needed twice as long to recover from it.

Inflation Continues after the War

The ink of the peace treaty was barely dry, returned soldiers almost reacclimated, and factories just reconverted to peacetime production by 1948, when tensions with the Soviets emerged and American defense officials began to operate on the premise that "peace could not be had ex-cept by arming as if for war." Businessmen, concerned that defense needs might interfere with consumer produc-tion, asked federal officials what economic and military co-operation might soon be required of them. Labor lead-ers expressed fears that national defense requirements and Marshall Plan economic aid commitments abroad might create severe inflation.

Inflation signs outpaced harbingers of depression. Three years after V-J Day, food prices had increased 50 percent, rent, 9 percent; and total living costs, almost 70 percent. Many blamed pent-up consumer demands and easy money for high prices. Others said that business, labor and government gave in to inflation. Businessmen assumed that wages would rise, and they could not lower prices without endangering profits. Labor leaders assumed prices would rise and that workers needed higher wages to meet those prices. Government lacked standardized wage and price policies and aimed to prevent strikes and slowdowns that would foster inflation. Instead, it often sanctioned inflationary settlements.

Amidst abrupt new awareness of atomic power and Soviet threats, Americans demanded peace. As postwar recession fears lingered and burdened them, they wanted secure prosperity. Fatigued from depression and war, they wanted both peace and prosperity. One or the other alone would not do. They looked to business, labor and government leaders as the only powers in society that seemed big enough to handle the awesome task.

Government aggrandizement through social and defense programs had accompanied national survival in hard times and war. The national crises modified earlier convictions that the market alone could regulate land, labor and capital with little government intervention, except to protect individual liberty and private property.

Government expenditures increased tenfold from 1940 to 1945. Nondefense spending by 1945 tripled that of any New Deal year. People accepted a much larger national debt as well as government activity in previously private domains. President Harry S Truman used executive prerogatives to make the United States the largest banker, insurance broker, utility company, warehouse operator, shipowner, truck fleet operator, landlord and tenant in the country. The federal government was also the largest owner and operator of dry-cleaning establishments, bakeries, livestock farms, nurseries, shoe-repair shops and ice-cream plants. It even made rum and false teeth.

The government initiated stronger co-operation between public, labor and management sectors. Balanced re-

lationships won approval as long as they enhanced predictability. No one promised to continue such co-operation
after the war.

Reconversion returned parachute makers to corset
manufacturing, radar-equipment specialists to radio production, and military-equipment manufactures to auto
making. The government repealed wartime taxes on excess
profits and individual incomes, releasing money for private
business expansion. Peace and prosperity, a weaker executive and stronger private leadership might turn public confidence back to the private sector. The Bargain confirmed
the possibility.

The Truman Era

Harry S Truman, who felt the weight of the sun, the
moon and the stars upon him when he took office as
president, labored in the shadow of a strong predecessor,
Franklin D. Roosevelt. He often sent flowers to the late
President's grave and deferred to his widow. But he also
wished to improve upon Roosevelt's performance. The
new president wanted to expand and continue New Deal
programs but he wished to get rid of some "tactless, con-
tentious" New Dealers. He thought he could make New
Deal programs more efficient if he re-organized government departments. He believed that he might "good fellow" rather than force congressmen into passing his liberal
programs.

New Dealers Harold Ickes, Henry Wallace, Henry
Morgenthau, Frances Perkins and James Byrnes resigned
or were fired. Truman liberals, lame-duck politicians,
"men on the make" and business failures replaced them.
Many resented this "cult of mediocrity" or "Missouri
gang," and disliked the president's inability to pass his reform legislation through a conservative Congress.

The backbone of FDR's coalition, 13 million immigrants
who came to America in 1900 to 1914 and suffered
through the depression, remained loyal Democrats.

Although relatively well-off, they retained underdog attitudes and provided Truman with needed urban pluralities.

New Dealers in new times pressed cautiously for social legislation to protect the weak. They wanted to increase Social Security benefits, increase minimum wage, and provide better education, medical insurance and public housing. Beneficiaries of the New Deal who moved into the middle class wanted to secure their own positions before they welcomed many newcomers. Many assumed, however, that FDR would have lived up to his promise to upgrade the position of blacks in society after the war, so they supported fair employment practices. They also believed government held ultimate responsibility for a smooth-running economy, full employment and labor-management peace.

Although Truman retained many of the late President's constituents, he did not enjoy the crisis consensus his predecessor commanded during the previous years.

On the one hand, "Old Dealers," with Robert Taft as spokesman, challenged from the right. They wanted to curb federal power, pare down bureaucracy, minimize relief, revive business prerogatives and tone down labor strength through legislation. Some considered the New Deal communistic. Others merely thought it unnecessary in prosperity. They considered business benevolence better for employees than union musclepower or social legislation. From the left, on the other hand, Newer Dealers, led by Henry Wallace, vigorously attempted to honor FDR's Economic Bill of Rights by using Keynesian economic principles to maintain full employment, lend federal money to small businesses, maintain wage stability, aid education, and provide agricultural price supports and federal crop insurance. They called for strong antitrust measures and a guaranteed annual wage.

They considered Truman too tough in relations with the Soviet Union. Truman's New Deal in a transformed America met more well defined political opposition than

Franklin Roosevelt had. Roosevelt had threaded his programs through recovery, and justified government spending as a pump-priming device for hard times. Truman needed new methods in an expanding economy with high employment and inflation.

"He looks active but goes nowhere. He appears happiest when able to make a dramatic show of activity, secure in the knowledge that nothing much is going to happen," one Truman observer said. Stalemates resulted when he raised all issues but settled none. Citizens shrugged off his performance with "To Err is Truman," but history may forgive him his holding action amidst emerging changes, new dangers and pervasive uncertainties.

A postwar intellectual undercurrent stifled strong executive and federal action. Some intellectuals questioned the sincerity of Americans who continued to condemn Japanese and German fascism after winning the war with concentrated industrial-military might, strong government action and intense national spirit. Too, insecurity about Communism's call for state power came home to roost by 1948. Loyalty boards investigated federal employees. Eleven key Red leaders faced trial for violating the Smith Act. Whittaker Chambers, a former Communist agent, repeated accusations against Alger Hiss before the House Un-American Activities Committee. McCarthyism's first flowering began to enervate public trust in government, and the times favored private initiatives.

"If we let inflation run away, the Russians will have won the Cold War without firing a shot," Truman announced. He talked tough about inflation but lost the support of Congress. The president had maintained wartime price controls until 1946. He vetoed a feeble price regulation measure voted by Congress in June of that year and found July's stronger measure difficult to administer. Widespread public support, needed to enforce wage and price controls, diminished in the peacetime economy.

Truman asked a special session of the predominantly Republican Congress for price controls on scarce products and wage ceilings to make price ceilings effective. Labor and business groups opposed his controls in part or in total. Michigan's Republican Representative Clare Hoffman thought Truman wanted a complete return to price control and rationing, knowing he would not win it. Then, Truman could blame Congress for the inflation.

Congress rushed its own "voluntary anti-inflation program" to the reluctant president, who signed it, believing the measure ineffectual. Under the program, federal agencies consulted industry and agriculture about priorities, allocation, conservation, inventory control and other forms of product regulation. They reached some voluntary agreements to relax antitrust laws. The combination of Hooverian voluntary government-business agreement and Rooseveltian co-operative government-business relaxation of antitrust laws did little to ameliorate inflation.

In January 1948, Truman offered a "cost-of-living tax program." Each taxpayer would gain forty dollars in cost-of-living credit, and forty dollars credit for each dependent. Federal revenue would decrease $3.2 billion, but higher corporate taxes would regain the loss. Congress buried the program and perfected its own, which reduced individual income taxes by $5.6 billion while avoiding penalties to corporations.

Corporations feebly tried to help. General Electric reduced prices 5 percent on 40 percent of its products. Ford Motor Company and International Harvester initiated price cuts, but rescinded them when their costs rose.

The president, who originally gained worker confidence, tried to resolve labor-management crises. Inflation had often fomented worker agitation for higher wages to match higher living costs, and agitation, in turn, had often fostered more inflation. Basically, Truman supported worker wage campaigns, but intervened in some postwar strikes. In the coal dispute, for example, he threatened government takeover of coal operations, and military service for pugnacious strikers. In contrast (or ironically), conservative (or business-oriented) Senator Robert Taft opposed such Draconian measures.

The co-operation of the big three economic sectors of

society broke down. Both labor and management tired of government impositions: depression years had seen the Blue Eagle and the Wagner Act; War years, War Labor Board and War Labor Disputes Act, and the postwar years, fact-finding committees and the Taft-Hartley Act. They began to suspect that government gained power from playing them against each other, and there was confusion over the legislation itself. For example, the Taft-Hartley Act of 1947 allegedly thwarted unfair labor practices much as the 1935 Wagner Act had attempted to end unfair management practices. At one extreme, National Labor Relations Board member Heber Blankenhorn resigned because he believed the 1947 law so harmful to labor organization that "even its own backers want its enforcement soft-pedalled." At the other extreme, workers surveyed by public-opinion researchers disapproved of the law by name. But, when asked whether they would approve specific measures which constituted the law, they registered an average 73 percent approval.

Each private sector had matured in its own way. Businessmen had been extravagant and wasteful in the 1920's, unpopular in the 1930's and had been tested by their voluntary co-operation with labor leaders, scientists, public officials and others during the war years. Corporate leaders approached the 1940's with more social caution, if not a social conscience. Workers who shut down plants with sit-down strikes in the late 1930's built their own homes in neat neighborhoods in the late 1940's. Full employment and wages, sometimes tripling depression wages, accounted for the change. More respect for private property resulted. At the same time, unions thrived under bureaucratic discipline and "lodge hall" fellowship. They increasingly turned to statistics to speak their minds and, more frequently, evicted Communists as menaces from within.

Enlightened industrial statesmen met establishment labor leaders in a new light by 1948. History gave the private sector its cue. The auto-industry actors, once backstage, were now ready to play their leading roles in The Bargain.

The audience would applaud cars, not conflict, and both the UAW and GM knew it. Prosperity was within reach if only workers won ample wages. . . if only company officials gained secure labor peace. . . if only prices did not soar. More than in any previous session, fellowship lured. After they aired all the arguments, accusations and justifications, the sounds of "if only" prevailed.

2

The United Auto Workers
From Sit-Down to Good Standing

LEADERS OF THE 1947 United Automobile Workers convention told delegates they belonged to the "largest free industrial union in the world," which by April 1948, claimed a record peacetime membership of nine hundred fifty thousand. During organizing years, federal legislation protected and fostered union recognition. After World War II, the UAW grew stronger internally because factionalism subsided and leaders played down Communist influences. Factional rivalries, previously hailed as "democracy in action," now threatened the unity with which Walter Reuther hoped to strengthen the UAW. Communists, once welcomed as fellow organizers, became enemies with divergent goals.

Walter Reuther

President Reuther's drive to power created and coincided with the unified strength the union presented in 1948. Reuther was a man of few vices and low pay, compared with other union officials. He did not drink or smoke—at cocktail parties he ordered Manhattans, ate the cherries and left the drink. The UAW president apparently showed no interest in women other than his wife, May, a former schoolteacher and Socialist who worked in Local 174 and raised their two daughters. He also accumulated no debts, and even engaged in conspicuous underconsumption. He often flew to United Automobile Workers conventions on cut-rate overnight air coach flights and squeezed his own orange juice in his hotel room at breakfast. When they travelled together, the Reuthers frequented family cafeterias and ordered specials.

In 1948 he earned $10,000, about half the salary of Steelworkers president Philip Murray and one-third the earnings of Teamster Union president Dan Tobin. Nearly every day he donned a seedy old balmacan-style top coat, left his five-room West Detroit bungalow furnished with much of his own carpentry, and drove his 1940 Chevrolet to his office for twelve hours of work.

If Reuther had any vices, they were that he chewed gum and craved power. He must have sensed that he needed power, not to enrich himself, but to reform society in ways he considered necessary. He won control of the union in order to institute reform, but he also instituted reforms in order to gain more power.

The four Reuther brothers inherited a legacy of socialism, rooted in grandfather Jacob Reuther's inclination for German democratic Marxism. At home in Wheeling, West Virginia, their father, Valentine Reuther, convened Ted, Walter, Victor and Roy for Sunday debates on economic and social topics. Victor and Walter carried on Socialist Worker Party (SWP) youth activities as students at Detroit's Wayne University in the early 1930's. After Ford Motor Company fired Walter on suspicion of Socialist activities, the brothers continued to explore workers movements abroad during the depression. While abroad, they narrowly escaped capture by Nazi police, and they worked in a Gorki, Russia automobile factory which the Ford Motor Company built for the Russians. Walter trained peasants in precise machinist work and won bonuses for his production ideas. When they returned to the U.S. in the fall of 1935, Walter ran for the office of Detroit councilman on the Socialist Party ticket and lost. By 1946, he publicly denounced socialism.

He was only twenty-six years old when he joined Detroit's Westside Local 174 of the United Automobile Workers and became their 1936 convention delegate. He and five others took shifts sleeping in their South Bend, Indiana hotel bed at the convention. One of Walter's stirring speeches prompted conventioneers to elect him to the UAW International Council.

The Reuthers won fellow worker confidence early, and spoke on labor problems and distributed handbills at factory gates until events precipitated their dramatic show of strength. On the basis of Local 174 member complaints of speedup at Detroit's Kelsey-Hayes plant, they carried out a "signal" sit-down strike in 1936. The strike inspired more labor protest in Flint, Michigan, where a sit-down which lasted almost two months ended in GM recognition of the UAW as the bargaining agent by General Motors. Local 174's membership soared from seventy-eight to thirty thousand in a few weeks.

UAW Factional Strife

UAW factional strife emerged in the year of the sit-down strike and lasted almost a decade until Reuther's unifying power won out. In 1937, Reuther joined with UAW secretary-treasurer George Addes and others to oppose then–UAW president Homer Martin, a former minister. Their anti-Martin bloc, called the Unity Caucus, believed that management was provoking workers with speedup and job discrimination and fomenting the minority of organized workers to a strike. Through these tactics the company expected to overwhelm and destroy the unity of the workers.

Instead, the strikes provoked more organization. Martin disliked the Unity Caucus's support of wildcat strikes, and did not join caucus members who went to the Ford

River Rouge plant May 26, 1937 to pass out handbills. There, Ford's hired thugs beat the Unity Caucus men—who gained widespread publicity when news photographers captured the incident. ·Thereafter, it was known as the "Battle of the Overpass." The Unity Caucus and other of Martin's enemies accused him of collusion with Ford officials.

Accusations, suspensions and desertions followed in 1938 and 1939. Martin suspended, reinstated and suspended again a group of five officers including Addes. The new faction met in Addes's apartment, held local union dues checks sent to them rather than to Martin, set up their own headquarters and held their own convention. With some Congress of Industrial Organizations support, the new caucus prevailed and the Martin group, backed by the American Federation of Labor, faded.

The seams of this victorious Unity Caucus weakened during World War II, as Reuther's power, growing from within the successful faction, challenged president R.J. Thomas, secretary-treasurer George Addes and their followers. Factionalism centered more on these personalities and their leadership struggles than on issues.

Ironically, Lutheran Walter Reuther allied with the Association of Catholic Trade Unionists (ACTU) in these early years, while Roman Catholic George Addes denounced the ACTU. Experts within Catholic parishes trained ACTU members in parliamentary order and obstructionist techniques, and they studied papal encyclicals on labor. Addes, not a Communist himself, continued to gain support from leftist elements he believed valuable to union-organizing goals.

By August 1941, at the Buffalo UAW Convention, Reuther was elected vice president, under Thomas as president and Addes as secretary-treasurer. Red-headed Reuther's ambitions and capabilities showed up in three crucial struggles that year. First, he sought to expel executive board member Lew Michener because he had led aircraft workers in a wildcat strike, which United States Army officials and some UAW leaders ended. Although few union convention members openly advocated wildcat strikes, they probably secretly admired Michener's actions as a revival of the 1930's union militance. A close vote, which prevented Michener's expulsion, favored the Addes faction but also showed Reuther a compentent opposition leader.

Second, Reuther tried to delay seating of the Allis-Chalmers union delegates because he considered them Communists. Addes won a strong point when he reminded delegates that the UAW constitution did not prevent officeholding on the grounds of either political or religious affiliations. Third, Reuther retaliated. He supported and won a constitutional amendment that denied Communists but permitted Socialists and Catholics to hold union offices.

The war issues of Addes and Reuther came into conflict at many points. CIO president John L. Lewis backed Addes's opposition to war in 1939, while Reuther and President Roosevelt advocated immediate conversion of the auto industry to war production and increased aid to Britain. Later, Reuther, Addes and even union Communists promoted labor unity to win the war at all costs in the "victory through equality of sacrifice" program.

When Reuther considered rescinding their no-strike pledge during the war, Addes's group accused him of a "strike and the war be damned" policy. Addes suggested incentive pay plans to promote war efforts, but Reuther disagreed and won rank-and-file support. He dramatized his patriotic war efforts when he took 250 shop stewards to a mock boot camp where they dug trenches, paddled assault boats and performed other military services.

He also spoke out constantly in the press, protesting government-agency wage ceilings, price control and inactivity on housing shortages. Reuther also accused employers of getting active unionists drafted under the aegis of "nonessential labor." In 1944, president R.J. Thomas, contrary to his friends' best advice, and over several executive board vetoes, appointed Walter Reuther chairman of the UAW's GM Department, a very important union post.

The position allowed the appointee to gain a reputation for strike activism in the 1945-46, 113-day GM-UAW skirmish. He focused the struggle on his economic argument that workers deserved a 30-percent wage increase to meet living-cost raises during the war. Other possible leaders blundered as Reuther thundered. Richard Frankensteen basked in sunny California while workers manned picket lines in Michigan's icy winter temperatures. UAW president R.J. Thomas tried an abortive "back to work" movement. Thomas, Addes and Frankensteen opposed the strike because retooling was incomplete and the steel supply was inadequate. They reasoned that a strike would not punish a company as much under these conditions.

The 18.5-cent increase the UAW accepted in March 1946 followed a pattern set in several other key industries that year. It fell below the 19.5-cent increase Truman's fact-finding board recommended which Reuther disavowed. It also fell far below Reuther's 30-percent wage-increase bid. Many deserted the strike activist in 1946, and his political future looked bleak. Meanwhile, Thomas and Addes held the two most important union posts and controlled a majority of the executive board members.

At the 1947 convention, the redhead's speeches and job offers in night-caucus sessions regained him some support. He evidently proposed to Addes a Thomas-Addes-Reuther race for UAW presidency, which they both expected Thomas to lose. Reuther suggested that he and Addes should support for secretary-treasurer the loser of a run-off race between the two of them. Addes refused. In the final hours of the 1946 UAW election, Reuther sent persuaders to hotels, barrooms, and railway stations to make sure that none of his voting supporters escaped. Because he needed more time than the two-hour roll call allowed to win uncommitted delegates, he questioned an unimportant constitutional point to create the needed delay. His opponents fell for the device. Thomas discussed the issue, and Reuther's planted speaker also took the floor. Nonsmoking Reuther peered through the smoke-filled room and determined when enough of his men had entered, and then he yielded the point. When the roll was called Reuther recorded a victory by a narrow 124-vote margin out of the 8674 votes tabulated. Thomas accepted a vice presidency and Addes won his tenth term as secretary-treasurer. Few members on the new executive board backed Reuther against the Thomas and Addes faction.

Reuther Consolidates His Power

As president he was isolated among enemies. Reuther's foes accused him of using "police state tactics," observing who ate lunch together and shared rides to the extent that members became discreet in expressing sympathies. Others thought Reuther ran the huge industrial union as a "well-oiled machine." He took advantage of the few positions his backers held in the union (the publications editor and education-department director posts, for example). His brother Victor held the latter office, through which he trained local leaders to take Walter's plans favorably to rank-and-file union members.

Reuther sought a deliberate public shedding of the UAW Communists, and opponents accused him of "red-baiting" and accusing even non-Communists of Red affiliation in order to weaken their union influence. Addes and most of his followers saw party members as minor influences in union politics and decisions, and appreciated their continued support from organizing days. They began "Reuther-baiting," calling him an ally of big business, a champion of the Taft-Hartley Act and a proponent of speedup in factories.

At about the same time, ninety thousand Farm Equipment (FE) workers proposed a merger with the UAW under terms quite favorable to themselves. They would be able to appoint certain executive board members and send delegates to the upcoming fall convention. Reuther believed that Communists strongly influenced the Farm Equipment members. He protested that the Farm Equipment merger proposal was unconstitutional and would make the FE a union within a union, with FE members getting special privileges. The Addes faction supported the merger, but agreed that all locals should vote on it. The locals voted "no" on the proposal, a victory for Reuther.

The most crucial Red-related issue concerned UAW acceptance or rejection of the Taft-Hartley Act provision. This required UAW members to sign affidavits that they were not Communists. Following an executive-board order, one hundred thousand auto workers left their jobs and marched to Cadillac Square in Detroit to protest the entire Taft-Hartley Law. A few locals, which Reuther evidently influenced, remained at work. Protesters later received company discharges or penalties. UAW member John Anderson, a protester at the time, remembered, "Here was another reminder to all of us of the left that we no longer had a union that would defend us as union members."

Addes considered the law unjust and unconstitutional, and CIO president Philip Murray backed him. Addes explained that if industry as well as labor had been required to sign non-Communist affidavits, he probably would not have seen anything wrong with it. But he sensed that the lawmakers were picking on labor. If a union did not comply, it lost National Labor Relations Board (NLRB) services.

Legal experts helped Reuther find a means to pressure the UAW Executive Board majority to comply with the Taft-Hartley provision. He directed UAW members to send an "intent to comply" statement to the NLRB so it would continue to hold elections and hearings for UAW members with cases pending. They could object to the law's "constitutionality, validity and applicability" at the end of their intent-to-comply forms. Reuther then promised to consider further rejection or acceptance of the law at the upcoming convention.

Members assumed that those who would not sign Taft-Hartley affidavits were Communists and therefore ineligible to hold union office. In that case the law helped Reuther control leadership positions.

The House Un-American Activities Committee subpoenaed witnesses and sought their affiliations. Many received letters, visits, or inquiries from the Immigration Department or the Federal Bureau of Investigation. Sometimes officials asked, "If you are not a Communist, why don't you support Walter Reuther?" Most of the two thousand delegates to the 1947 UAW convention applauded Reuther's slogan, "Resent and Reject Communism." It helped him renew his presidency and win twenty of the twenty-two executive board positions. Reuther's opposition faltered and its leaders went elsewhere: Addes into the nightclub business and R.J. Thomas into a minor CIO position. The victorious UAW ruler warned auto-company officials that they should not try to exploit union factions because there would be none in the future.

The newly unified UAW began to strengthen itself financially. After three months in office, secretary-treasurer Emil Mazey reported a $330,000 surplus. By January 1948, with their strike fund approaching $750,000, Mazey called for a five- to six-million-dollar strike fund to improve their bargaining position. Members paid their one dollar yearly dues in March, and the fund neared $2 million. Campaigns in GM plants in February and March won twenty-five to thirty thousand new UAW members.

The largest United States industrial union hinted of its emergent forcefulness in American politics as its president and political action committee (PAC) discussed issues favoring certain candidates in 1948, a presidential-election year. In early 1948, the Republicans dominated Michigan politics, but James R. Hoffa used Teamster funds to control the Michigan Democratic Party machinery. The UAW's potential for political influence in Michigan surfaced in spite of Hoffa's activities. Wayne County, where UAW members and their wives accounted for 60 percent of registered voters, sent 40 percent of the Michigan delegates to the Democratic convention.

The leader whose ascendancy united and strengthened the UAW by 1948 did more than anyone else to create the setting for The Bargain. Unfortunately, he was temporarily sidelined.

On April 20, 1948, Reuther came home late from an executive board meeting at the Book-Cadillac Hotel in Detroit. While he was eating a late meal and talking with his wife about their children, four shotgun blasts broke through their kitchen window and hit him in the right arm and chest. He fell to the floor. While his wife administered first aid, a neighborhood boy saw a man make a getaway in a 1947 or 1948 maroon Ford sedan. Although officials offered $112,600 for the gunman's capture, they never found the assailant. Reuther was rushed to Grace Hospital, where he recuperated for most of the remainder of the bargaining session with GM. The following spring, another gunman shot Victor Reuther. In retrospect, observers said both shootings made it difficult for anyone to criticize the Reuthers. Walter's shooting martyred him among his members, which would possibly cause UAW members to fight harder if it came to a strike. This attack on Walter Reuther distracted reporters from conjecture about events transpiring behind closed doors of the bargaining room.

For many years Walter Reuther clutched a ball in his right hand to exercise the arm that had been shot. The man who gave the union its strong right arm by 1948 allowed the contract setting he helped to create run on its own power.

3

General Motors
The Wheels of Fortune

SOME UAW LEADERS characterized General Motors, the nation's largest manufacturing company, as "a corporation with its headquarters in Wall Street and hindquarters spread all over the world."

People expected giants like GM to "look little and do big things." Shareholders wanted higher profits; consumers, more and better cars; and workers, high wages. Threats of antitrust suits lingered and labor unions cited generous profits as a reason for receiving higher wages. Ford, the third largest manufacturing company in the United States; Chrysler, the fifth; American Motors, the 113th, and six other postwar carmakers schemed to overtake GM or to cut into its market share. New entrants into the industry dreamed of taking advantage of enormous consumer demand, and marketed innovative products.

Postwar Uncertainties

Speculations which darkened the brightest predictions of prosperity also threatened GM: export and domestic demand might slacken; Marshall Plan requirements might divert raw materials needed in auto manufacturing; new cars might be too expensive for workers and farmers who had spent most of their wartime savings; families with incomes adequate to buy new cars would resist spending if a recession occurred. Long strikes, like the 1945-46 GM-UAW strike, might inflate wages and prices even more. General Motors, capitalism's winner, always had more to gain—and more to lose. The company made more cars than anyone in the world. If people bought, GM sold. If people balked, the company had more cars unsold, and more money to lose. UAW officials selected GM as their first target because the union believed the company had the most money available for wages and would rather pay than fight.

Ford, the leading automobile manufacturer in the early days of the industry, was overtaken by GM, by the 1930's; Chrysler ran a strong second for several years. The Big Three (Ford, Chrysler, and GM) dominated the market in 1948, but seven other smaller companies increased their share of sales. To compete, car companies improved products, introduced new ideas, anticipated consumer tastes and used aggressive advertising and salesmanship. Formal price-fixing was illegal, but price leadership, with GM the keystone, helped minimize that area of competition, especially after the early 1950's. GM, with about 40 percent of the market, calculated new costs and set new prices to meet their own historical average profit margin at standard volume. With the price set, Chrysler and Ford, each with about 20 percent of the market, tried to match GM. Generally they did not come up with profit margins comparable to General Motors. Smaller companies, which went from a prewar 10 percent to postwar 20 percent market share, followed a similar pattern.

Cost increases greatly influenced immediate postwar pricing, as labor, steel, glass, upholstery and other materials increased in cost. Advertising campaigns sounded even more vicious than pricing competition. The automobile companies hinted of "extraordinary but as yet top-secret" campaigns in early 1948. They promised that only the strongest advertisers would survive the struggle.

In 1948, and until about 1952, pent-up demand overshadowed GM's latent price leadership or advertising wars in automobile competition. General Motors made its historical profit margin and its dealers made more than their normal profit share. From October 1945 through 1947, to avoid dealer charges of favoritism, GM allocated cars to its dealers based on their 1941 sales performances. Consumer demand remained so great that Chrysler, Ford and others could price their comparable models higher than those of General Motors and still sell them. They also were able to cut some other prices without starting a price war with GM.

Newspaper articles frequently compared high postwar prices with those of the lower prewar period. Automobile firms wanted to avoid public censure, excessive wage demands or antitrust suits, so they curbed prices somewhat and allowed their dealers to get the best of profits. Dealers deflated trade-in values, loaded cars with "extras" and demanded kickbacks. They received a 30 percent return on the net worth of their cars. Used cars in this period sometimes sold for more than their original cost. Some unscrupulous dealers bought brand-new cars from consumers and sold them at a profit to new customers or used-car dealers. There were cases in which dealers hired "spotters" who took up stations at stop lights waving $100 bills at passing motorists whose cars looked promising for resale. Many casual entrepreneurs joined new- and used-car dealers in this "new-used car" business. Frustrating and fierce competition ensued. As one auto executive recalled, "It was an Alice-In-Wonderland" period, in which no one could keep up with the demand.

Such excessive demand meant that those who started auto companies could produce at less-than-efficient scale and still profit. They need not fight so hard to sell, nor worry greatly about the effect of their pricing on other companies. The government sold war surplus factories and machine tools at bargain prices, which helped entrants into the field. Prosperous dealers and eager customers lured potential dealers into accepting any franchises—even ones for new companies.

New automobile companies planned attention-catching models such as three wheelers, midget cars, flying models and light weight autos. The Playboy, for example, was billed as "The Nation's Newest Car Sensation." Built in Buffalo, New York between 1946 and 1951 by the Playboy Motor Car Corporation, this compact three-seater convertible sold for nine hundred and eighty-five dollars. Another postwar model, the Tucker, named for its designer, Preston T. Tucker, stressed safety and included disc brakes, a padded dashboard, a front passenger crash compartment and a popout windowscreen. The Tucker Torpedo, a sports model and the Tucker Sedan were manufactured in Chicago between 1946 and 1948. Plans for a central steering wheel and iron wings that turned with the wheels were shelved by company managers, but they did retain the three headlights that had been introduced on the original Tucker Torpedo. The car stood a little over five feet high, had a ten foot, eight inch wheelbase, and weighed 3,600 pounds.

Cost advantages, economies of scale, brand name reputation and product differentiation helped the established auto firms outdo new entrants. Also model changes and curved windshields helped eliminate less well-capitalized companies which could not afford expensive retooling.

In 1948—the year the one hundred millionth motor vehicle came off the assembly line—the Big Three auto companies (General Motors, Ford, Chrysler) announced the first new postwar auto designs. (Previous postwar cars had been "face-lifted" 1942 styles.) The 1948 Cadillac introduced tail fins. Harley Earl, son of a carriage-maker and GM's vice president of styling, got the inspirtation for tail fins as he viewed the P-38 fighter plane. At first the idea was difficult to sell, but it fostered the impulse toward the "longer, lower and lovelier" postwar cars endorsed by Hollywood stars. Automobiles with three tones of paint enlivened the highways at the same time. Prior to the late 1940's automobile makers customarily changed car bodies every four or five years, with "face-lifts" between. A shorter cycle of changes gained favor as styling became more important in competition.

Progressively bigger, higher-compression engines started the horsepower competition that would continue for years. In 1948 General Motors introduced the first high-compression V-8 engines. Buick offered the first torque-converter type automatic transmission in a U.S. passenger car.

After the war, both GM and Ford thought people wanted smaller, lighter and cheaper cars. The federal government approved a new GM plant for small car manufacture. By September 1948, both companies dashed their plans, because factory building failed and materials remained too scarce. Besides, buyers did not want to give up the luxuries of current car models, and GM figured that it could sell the projected small car for only one hundred dollars less than its popular Chevrolet. GM salvaged small car developmental progress through its manufacture of the Australian Holden.

Among other U.S. companies, Nash Motors (now part of American Motors Corporation) built a small version of the Rambler; Hudson made a small Hornet; and Kaiser-Frazer Corporation introduced its Henry J, a small four-cylinder car with a base price of $1,295. Meanwhile, in 1948 the Volkswagen "Beetle" began to invade the American market, after two GI's who had served in Germany brought their VW's home.

General Motors Stays on Top

General Motors topped Ford in these years because of Ford's shortcomings and because from the late 1920's it remained more successfully integrated than Ford. GM had acquired significant and useful subsidiaries, such as Fisher Body Corporation and accessories divisions. The company had begun aircraft and diesel-engine production with the idea that they might learn something useful if they needed to make war material. General Motors avoided buying unrelated industries, such as prefabricated housing, and produced more of its own major components than others did, providing replacement parts in the U.S. and foreign truck and car markets. The General Motors Acceptance Corporation, a subsidiary, financed its own products. Another subsidiary, Motors Insurance Corporation, insured company-financed cars. GM owned Frigidaire, which made home appliances, diesel locomotives, industrial and marine diesel engines, earth-moving machinery, gas turbines and heavy-duty transmissions. At one time, the company owned Hertz Driveurself Corporation as well as minority shares in bus, aviation, chemical and gasoline corporations.

General Motors thrived on its semi-centralized organization, with five car divisions ultimately controlled through financial and administrative policies at central headquarters. Multiple models in each of the car divisions gave market flexibility. All their hopes were not placed on one horsepower. Winners balanced losers.

Unlike Ford, GM protected itself against disintegration at the end of a life cycle of crucial company men. Ford had been dominated by Henry Ford, Sr. and a few others. Death and retirement without suitable replacements was a significant factor which allowed GM to overtake Ford during this period until a postwar change in Ford management occured. Too, GM had attracted and kept able employees when they adopted a bonus plan and Manager Security Plan in the 1920's.

Before 1933, GM had no formal policy or department which determined labor relations. Section 7a of the National Industrial Recovery Act (NIRA) of 1933 legitimized collective bargaining and spurred industrial union organization. The resultant unions clashed with company-encouraged employee associations. In 1934, GM President Alfred P. Sloan endorsed collective bargaining and continued to do so after a Supreme Court decision nullified the NIRA in 1935.

Management recognized the United Automobile Workers as the exclusive bargaining agent for its members after the sit-down strike of 1937, and in 1940 the National Labor Relations Board certified the UAW-CIO as the bargaining agent for *all* GM workers. GM and the UAW negotiated their first agreement in 1937. Nevertheless, in those early years, wildcat strikes continued and factionalism made it difficult for the company to decide which faction was the actual bargaining agent.

During World War II, both GM and the UAW representatives turned to the National War Labor Board to help resolve their disputes. After the war, the UAW held up GM production for 113 days and held out for a thirty percent wage increase which was never received. Some GM officials complained of the "shotgun wedding" between labor and management in depression and war years, but GM acknowledged unions as a permanent force and sought to contain them on terms acceptable to both parties.

Postwar GM representatives told a senate labor committee that the company no longer used "thugs, spies, tear gas or bullying techniques in industrial labor warfare." The Taft-Hartley Act seemed to some GM officials a needed protection of companies from labor excesses. By 1948, with management tired of going in and out of negotiations, a longer, sounder agreement was sought so executives could concentrate on other business problems.

This goal was foremost in the mind of GM president Charles Erwin Wilson. Wilson sensed that to gain labor peace, corporate officials needed to acknowledge worker strengths. Privately, one GM executive allegedly said,

"Why let the bureaucrats and labor bosses twist our arm? Let's get back to free enterprise."Wilson responded, "Yes, I guess you're right, but after all, here we are now."

Engine Charlie Wilson

For a man who moved with the times, time often caught up with Wilson. Once GM's labor-relations staff member Louis Seaton took a memorable three-week trip with the company president. They had to ask the New York Central Railroad to hold the train to New York in Windsor, Ontario until Wilson arrived. Another time, they somehow managed to board the Cleveland-to-Buffalo boat after sailors had taken up the gangplank.

Seaton recalled, "He would get so engrossed in what he was discussing that time slipped by until someone would courageously interrupt, 'C.E., do you know that it is nine o'clock and I'm getting hungry.' " He added, "When we finally got to bed at night he would tell us, 'When you go to breakfast, wake me up and order the same thing you get, and I will be there to eat it.' "

Wilson probably never forgot his humble beginnings. His father had been principal of a Minerva, Ohio school where his mother also taught. Young Wilson quickly made friends when the family moved to Mineral City, Ohio. The town blacksmith let him work the bellows and hand him the tongs. A town section hand allowed him to run a handcar on a siding. He sometimes rode with locomotive engineers. A schoolmate's father, a coal miner, let them load coal. He also lingered at the local light plant and stoked boilers, trying to find out about electricity and how generators worked.

Wilson applied his technical curiosities to schoolwork, graduating from a Pittsburgh high school at sixteen and finishing a four-year course in three years at Carnegie Tech. He made filament lamps for twelve cents an hour to pay for his schooling. Westinghouse Corporation hired him as a student engineer apprentice in 1909. As his salary almost tripled after three years of work there, he decided he could afford to marry Jessie Ann Curtis. They raised chickens and garden vegetables to feed their children.

Before World War I, Wilson helped Westinghouse's genius designer B.G. Lamme convert concepts to mathematical formulas, simplify processes and improve equipment design. He designed the first auto starters for Westinghouse and supervised their auto electrical equipment engineering just as those operations were in their most competitive and experimental stages.

The government drafted him in World War I. He designed radio generators, made a primitive crystal set (precursor to the walkie-talkie), invented a generator to attach to the wing of a 1918 airplane and made Army B truck electrical equipment.

After World War I, he joined the Delco Corporation, a GM subsidiary, and later became its chief engineer and sales manager. He so improved Delco factory operations in Anderson, Indiana by introducing new designs that their sales problems vanished. As president of the merged Delco-Remy Corporation in Dayton, Ohio, he saved the company $5 million annually when he consolidated ignition work, and he assigned displaced employees to new tasks. In 1929, GM named him vice president of their accessories division, and ten years later he was appointed vice president. Wilson chaired the committee negotiating GM's first union contract because then–GM President William Knudsen thought Wilson talked more than Knudsen did and had more patience. Wilson ignored his associates who thought the way to handle union business was to "pay off somebody."

Knudsen resigned from the presidency of General Motors in 1941 to serve the federal government and Wilson replaced him. He remained as president of General Motors until 1953, when President Eisenhower appointed him Secretary of Defense.

A Horatio Alger success story himself, Wilson personified the corporation in those terms, claiming that to the degree that big business followed the "homely virtues of industry, thrift and honesty," it prospered.

Wilson certainly adhered to his principles and he himself prospered. Personal records in 1946 show his worth to be $5,145,140.79. Only $5,000 of this money was invested in automobiles and $1,500 in horses. He, his wife and their six children held stocks, real estate and insurance policies. His charity ranged from a two-dollar check to an old schoolmate for tobacco, to $2,500 for the political campaign of a friend. By 1949, he ranked as the highest paid corporate executive in the United States, earning $586,100 in salary, bonus and stock and paying about $430,350 in taxes.

People accepted simple, open-hearted practical idealism when it came from this wealthy head of the world's richest corporation. In later years, he was mistakenly immortalized as the man who quipped, "What's good for General Motors is good for the country." A senator in hearings concerning his nomination for Secretary of Defense asked him whether he could serve the best interests of the government in situations where there could be adverse effects to his GM stockholdings. Wilson replied, "Yes sir, I could." Then he qualified, "I honestly cannot conceive of one [such situation] because for years I thought that what was good for our country was good for General Motors and vice versa." He went on to explain that because GM was big, its welfare coincided with the nation's and the company contributed in turn to the country's welfare.

Business associates attested to his simple sincerity. Stephen DuBrul, who helped Wilson write speeches for more than ten years, commented that Wilson "wrote from his heart," imploring them to correct his grammar and clarify his expression, while appreciating their understanding and lack of contention. He told them once, "What I'm going to say is what I mean, and I simply want you to help me make clear to people what I mean." These same associates marveled at the sophistication of his economic thinking, attributing it to Wilson's years at Delco-Remy, when he sold products in competitive markets outside the corporation and went beyond simply running the plant.

Wilson believed that federal government policies controlled or caused inflation, especially policies concerning taxes, budget balancing, banks and credit institutions. Money supply was at the heart of inflation. Secondarily, he thought producers determined available goods and services and customers determined their turnover. Individual and corporate savings habits also influenced the picture.

Reduced wages and profits easily led to deflation, while increased wages and profits led to inflation, he concluded. Furthermore, he qualified, wage increases would not be inflationary if productivity increased proportionately. He believed, along with many labor leaders, Communists and government officials that "it is not primarily wages that push up prices. It is primarily prices that pull up wages."

Wilson and Reuther

Wilson and Reuther, both unorthodox leaders within their respective fields, developed an unusual mutual admiration for each other, fraught with the expected emnity, but evincing enough respect on both sides so that each learned from the other. Veteran Detroit labor reporter Jack Crellin believes that Reuther "indoctrinated" Wilson with social-conscience ideas at the bargaining table and public hearings. The GM president probably impressed his UAW counterpart with practical considerations.

During World War II, Wilson belonged to a ten-man labor-management committee, which the Office of Production Management (OPM) authorized to work out the conversion of automobile plants to war production. Reuther became known as special assistant to Sidney Hillman, who headed OPM with GM's William Knudsen. In these capacities the two leaders worked together in government wartime service.

Their mutual respect evidently showed in their debate over the World War II conversion policy, held in the GM building. The industrialist thought auto companies should use up their $200 million materials inventory in building 250,000 new cars, and then meet war production goals with the same efficient energy automobile companies used for their own peacetime goals. Reuther advocated quick war conversion, and a "socialistic" pooling of manpower and equipment through a single, government-labor-management planning board. He advocated that America build five hundred planes daily, and four million cars yearly. Newspaper reporters expected Reuther to win the debate, but both leaders proved themselves lively, convincing speakers, and the contest ended in a draw.

The Office of Price Management rejected Reuther's scheme as impractical, and events proved the judgment sensible. The standard fighter plane Reuther's plan would have created probably would have fallen short of technological and defense needs. The excessive number of cars he projected would have interfered with the contribution automobile plants made in producing tanks, heavy duty trucks, armored cars, airplane engines, gliders, carrier aircraft, diesel horsepower, machine guns and carbines as well as cooking pots, helmets, air-raid sirens and pontoon bridges.

Mutual respect grew greater in later years when events forced them to compromise because both were basically committed to capitalism and to moderation in politics. Reuther said he feared extreme reaction on the left and right would work together against the "democratic middle in world politics." Wilson hoped to do his part to save the nation from "the poison of extremes from either right or left."

The "gentleman" union leader wanted GM to be the most prosperous company in the automobile industry because "nothing could be more asinine than to destroy GM and the job opportunities with GM." The company president, who earned about sixty times as much as Reuther, took unusual interest in worker well-being. He gave reporters this characteristic "foot-in-mouth" opinion of his labor adversary: "Reuther is a remarkable leader, a very valuable man. . . I cannot tell you how good a man he is because his membership might not like it."

By 1948, Wilson probably anticipated GM's eventual price leadership and considered recent entrants in the industry a minor nuisance. He foresaw that GM's steadiest and most profitable course would be to maximize production, accurately or closely estimate labor costs and meet high consumer demand. To do so, the company needed to secure labor peace and longer term contracts. He welcomed a policy that would avoid much of the mystery and disruption of continual bargaining. Wilson would have to convince the board of directors and finance staff members that a productivity increase which he held would certainly come in a time of eager consumers and uninterrupted working days, could pay GM's wages, higher supply costs and taxes. New costs could not force prices up and result in volume and employment cuts because productivity and consumer demand would pay the bill, he insisted. GM needed to substantiate this argument to satisfy the UAW as much as its own finance staff.

The UAW had to maintain a delicate balance. Officials knew the company wanted maximum production and they could cripple GM with a strike which would benefit its competitors, but they also knew that a strike would affect the same workers who had just begun to recover financially from the long 1946 strike. The UAW was in a better position than before to balance options because it was more sure of its identity and unity than ever before. Tension between AFL and CIO factions no longer harmed the UAW.

The ambitious young redhead saw that the small percentage of Communists who once helped the workers organize was now a big liability to unity. The public might allow even greater union repression than the Taft-Hartley Act implied if the UAW insisted on continued close relations with Communists. The general political goals which the UAW stressed and the methods of the Reds did not mesh well with practical, economic drives channeled through collective bargaining and strikes. Reuther probably sensed that longer periods of high employment and rising membership during industrial prosperity would strengthen the union more than stubborn militance. Still, he needed to take a strong position to maintain his own power and gain advantages for UAW members.

The best position for Reuther and the UAW was probably to avoid internal political disruption and gnaw at, but not bite off, the hand that fed them. The union did not want to destroy General Motors; they wanted to get the best of it.

The UAW acted with more self-assurance, once the fight for recognition and unity ended successfully. Now, members sensed that if they worked for practical gains to strengthen their economic position, they might soon widen the scope of collective bargaining, maximize wages and seek new gains such as insurance benefits and pension programs. If their union prospered in membership and financial backing, they might even pursue political and social programs.

GM negotiators knew that UAW members wanted wages to keep up with living costs as well as to improve their standard of living. In spite of Taft-Hartley legislation, the elimination of Communist influence from the UAW and the emergence of a leader who talked friendship with GM, the UAW wielded considerable power. It might stop or delay vital production. General Motors did not want to destroy the union but desired rather to rationalize labor relations into more predictable patterns, so that the company might function effectively in a promising economy. By 1948, prosperity beckoned both parties to find a common meeting ground. If they could only find a principle to agree upon, the bargaining table was ready.

4

Ideas to Be Bargained With

THE STAGE WAS SET, the actors cast and the play had been written. Lord Keynes once said that nothing is so powerful as an idea whose time has come. The idea of the escalator clause in labor negotiations was not a new one, but until this time it was merely a concept in the minds of various theorists and not one which could easily be acted upon.

Leon Trotsky in his transitional program from capitalism to socialism, several foreign countries in halting experiments, the United States government in the "Little Steel Formula" during World War II, former GM president Alfred Sloan and now GM President "Engine Charlie" Wilson promoted some form of wage escalation. There was some history on which to base this seemingly radical idea.

Early Experiments in Escalation

Cost-of-living data shaped a few early labor decisions, if informally. In England, as early as 1707, a Cambridge don estimated price changes over six hundred years to determine comparable limits on outside income that fellowship scholars might receive. In the United States, cost-of-living considerations helped settle the 1902 anthracite coal strike, and influenced subsequent government arbitrated settlements. Frederick W. Taylor, the "scientific management" genius, thought cost-of-living wage adjustment would prevent union organization. The Bureau of Labor Statistics, developed during World War I, spurred a 1920's fascination with living-cost data. At the end of that decade prices dropped from their peaks, and workers stressed broader wage considerations because they feared cost of living settlements might freeze real wages.

Foreign countries reported some failures and some successes with their more formal escalation attempts during the 1920's. They were on a countrywide, rather than companywide, basis. Chile, in 1928, increased wages every year by a percentage equal to the previous year's cost of living increase. Wages increased 8,254 percent in twenty years. As a result, tax reform was initiated, government spending reduced and the pace of escalation was cut in half. Denmark, Belgium, Luxembourg, Italy and Great Britain all began to link wages and salaries to cost-of-living indices in the 1920's. But none of these arrangements tied wages to productivity. Cost-of-living wage adjustment eventually extended to private and public employment and to social security benefits in many European countries. Britain became disillusioned with the concept, whereupon its retail price index became merely a suggested tool for wage settlement. Compared with subsequent American programs, most foreign programs required a much larger surge of living costs before activation.

As World War II defense programs accelerated living costs, numerous United States contracts included escape clauses in order that wage adjustment might be reevaluated according to increased living costs without disturbing other points of agreement. The National War Labor Board decreed such clauses illegal (as in the "Little Steel Formula" of October, 1942) whenever escalated wages exceeded 15 percent of average straight time hourly rates prevailing on January 1, 1941. The 15-percent figure served as a ceiling for most wages except for textile workers compensation, which remained substandard. John L. Lewis, United Mine Workers president thought the percentage restrictive and rallied unsuccessfully for wage compensation perpetually tied to living-cost increases. Lewis's intransigence alienated Congress, which passed the War Labor Disputes Act, empowering the president to seize a struck war plant. This act was used twice against Lewis's coal miners during the war.

The National War Labor Board rejected an American Federation of Labor attempt to extend the escalation ceiling to 22 percent. Thereafter, most wage demands based on cost-of-living increases dwindled.

Small scale, temporary experiments in escalation occured at a Sinclair Oil facility and among Massachusetts shoe manufacturers in 1946, and in International Shoe Company and Shatterproof Glass Corporation contracts in 1947. Some UAW officials cited the oil company example to show worker dissatisfaction with escalation by 1947. Local union spokesmen at the Shatterproof Glass Corporation signed their escalation agreement with misgivings. But they felt justified when the UAW claimed its victory with the 1948 Bargain. The glass company pact covered three hundred salaried and hourly-rated workers for two years, but did not include an annual improvement factor.

Interest by Sloan and Wilson in Escalation

As early as 1935, GM president Alfred P. Sloan, Jr. considered adjusting GM's wages to cost-of-living increases. The long-faced, keen executive thought that GM would base wage adjustment on the Bureau of Labor Statistics index for individual cities, rather than for the nation as a whole. GM had plants in 12 of the thirty two cities for which the BLS published figures, and the company hired National Industrial Conference Board representatives to compute cost-of-living indices in GM plant cities which had not been studied by the government or by the NICB. Difficulty obtaining indices covering all GM plants and relatively stable consumer prices between 1935-40 discouraged the project.

By 1941, the defense program stimulated sharp price increases, and the new GM president Wilson considered responses while he recuperated in the hospital from a broken hip suffered in a skating accident. The economic picture and his desire to be useful motivated him to reconsider his predecessor's original interest in escalation. He believed GM should pioneer wage escalation because if only small companies tried it, no one would ever hear about it. He understood, however, that the UAW might fear wage escalation because it might keep real wages at a status-quo level.

Wilson invited GM executives Stephen DuBrul and Andrew Court to his Harper Hospital room to discuss and research wage matters. Some associates viewed tall, inquisitive Court as a corporate maverick or eccentric genius. (Successful cattle hide market predictions earned him an outstanding reputation before his GM career began. Too, Wilson was impressed by Court's paper on "hedonic horse power" which conceptualized a method of adjusting consumer-price and other economic indices for product-quality changes.) In 1941 Wilson summoned Court to Detroit to help him consider cost-of-living wage adjustment.

Court's superior and friend, bespectacled Stephen DuBrul, had gained respect for financial factors in business from his father, an econometrics pioneer of the 1920's. After joining General Motors in 1927, the younger DuBrul warned top management of a prolonged depression which would end in a banking collapse.

Getting Down to Specifics

While some executives sneaked steak dinners into the hospital for Wilson, DuBrul and Court quietly conveyed their discoveries and opinions on the questions he had asked them to research. He directed them to check the validity of the Consumer Price Index, and discern whether or not the union could divert it to their ends. They recognized that the Bureau of Labor Statistics cost-of-living index used statistics from families with lower incomes than GM's average worker. They discussed what index GM might use and how to construct their own cost-of-living formula.

The three considered local adjustment by cities, using National Industrial Conference Board indices for GM plant cities which the BLS indices did not cover. They asked themselves how often wages should be adjusted, and whether wages should be based on an average, the lowest wage or each individual worker's wage. For example, if the CPI increased about 2 percent, should a three-dollar-per-hour worker and a five-dollar-per-hour worker each get 2 percent of four dollars or should they get an adjustment in proportion to their own wages? The GM men decided to use an average wage base shunning local adjustment by cities, and selecting the national BLS CPI as their basis of adjustment. If a local index were used, Wilson projected that GM would end up giving increases to some workers and not to others, perhaps creating greater disturbances than ever. They evaluated that errors of deviation between cities would not make significant differences in formulating a nationwide consumer-price index. They thought a larger-scale survey would neutralize the possible effects of merchant estimations deliberately given to prompt wage increases. Furthermore, the BLS CPI was the most comprehensive at the time, and the union would probably refuse an NICB index because the compilation was financed by industry.

DuBrul thought the addition of productivity-based wages to escalated wages came as an afterthought to Wilson—something to assure his main goal, long-term contracts. The executives pondered how to measure productivity and relate it to wages. Court mentioned that if figures were available, the negotiators might have rendered the productivity factor for an individual plant, for General Motors only, for the automobile industry or on the basis of all American manufacturing. Or, they might have chosen historical averages or current achievement figures.

Court urged Wilson to base productivity increases on individual plants for the current period, making it a group bonus of sorts. He later recanted, "I think 'C.E.' quite rightly felt that the UAW wouldn't accept that. . . that gets back to piece rates."

Productivity figures for General Motors were not available, and its measurement proved difficult, especially compared with cost-of-living tabulations. Often, improved output per man-hour results from better supplies or improved machinery, rather than from the worker on the line.

Available studies indicated that each generation, or forty years, productivity doubled. They extrapolated that the country's productivity improved annually from seven-eights of one percent to 3 percent. They agreed to base the annual improvement factor (AIF) on 2 percent average annual historical national productivity. Wilson insisted that these factors be the only wages ever added to the projected cost-of-living allowance. DuBrul cautioned Wilson that "when the union boys signed up on the concepts, they would only stay with the formula as long as it seemed politically feasible," and he warned him union men would eventually demand more.

As DuBrul recalled, Wilson remarked, "Well, they mustn't do that. . . that's all there is to wack up. Anything beyond that would be inflationary." Wilson hoped that government and industry policy would support their 2-percent limits. He scolded DuBrul. "Your view of it is that this is just expediency." (DuBrul agreed.) "This isn't just expediency, it's a fundamentally sound document."

Reaction of Business to Escalation Concepts

A month or two after these three executives formulated more secure ideas, board chairman Sloan asked National Industrial Control Board director Virgil Jordan his opinion of wage escalation for GM and U.S. industry in

Charles Erwin Wilson. *General Motors Public Relations Library.*

Leon Trotsky in exile in France, 1934. *Archives of Labor and Urban Affairs, Wayne State University.*

Alfred P. Sloan, Jr. *General Motors Public Relations Library.*

Sit-down strike, GM plant, Flint, Michigan, 1937. *Archives of Labor and Urban Affairs, Wayne State University.*

Fisher Body Plant, Flint, Michigan, during 1937 sit-down strike. *Archives of Labor and Urban Affairs, Wayne State University.*

UAW organizers approached by Ford men in Dearborn, Michigan, May 26, 1937. Moments later the Ford men attacked the organizers in what became known as the "Battle of the Overpass." Walter Reuther is third from right. *Archives of Labor and Urban Affairs, Wayne State University.*

UAW organizer Richard Frankensteen being beaten at the "Battle of the Overpass," Dearborn, Michigan, May 26, 1937. *Archives of Labor and Urban Affairs, Wayne State University.*

General Motors Building, Detroit. *General Motors Public Relations Library.*

General Motors officials celebrating the production of GM's 25,000,000th automobile, January 1940. To the left of the vehicle are Harlow H. Curtice and Charles S. Mott; to the right of the car stand M. E. Coyle, William S. Knudsen, Alfred P. Sloan, Jr., and C. E. Wilson. *General Motors Public Relations Library.*

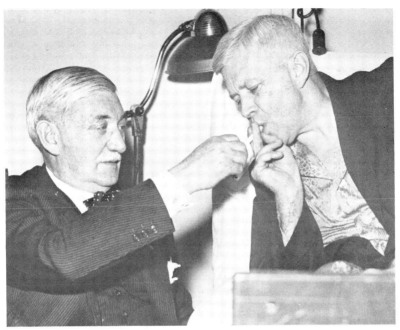

William S. Knudsen visits C. E. Wilson in hospital, February 1941. *Charles Erwin Wilson Archives.*

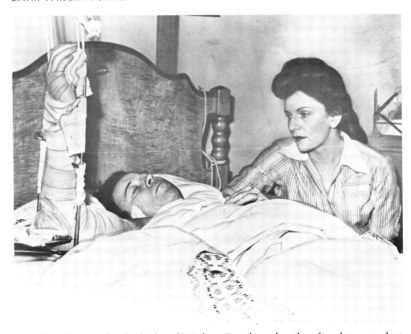

May Reuther at the bedside of Walter Reuther shortly after he was shot, Detroit, 1948. *Archives of Labor and Urban Affairs, Wayne State University.*

Walter Reuther speaking to a Labor Day rally, Detroit, 1948. *Archives of Labor and Urban Affairs, Wayne State University.*

Representatives of GM and the UAW reached agreement on the contract May 25, 1948. Left to right are John W. Livingston and T. A. Johnstone of the UAW, and Harry W. Anderson and Louis Seaton of GM. *United Press International.*

general. Jordan penned a discouraging reply. He assessed that labor wanted to gain political control of industry and economic organization so it might legislate rather than lobby or collective bargain for improved worker status. Since labor did not yet enjoy thorough political control at the time, Jordan predicted that labor unions would probably continue to bargain or strike for higher wages and shorter hours, and refuse automatic wage adjustment. Once they gained political control, labor leaders would need continued unionized worker votes. Workers would then reject cost-of-living allowances and seek higher wages and shorter hours regardless of their effect on real living standards.

In Jordan's judgment, a labor government might eventually accept these allowances if applied throughout all industry, providing the government controlled wages, working hours, prices and capital investment for each specific industry and operation. In any case, a rational automatic wage adjustment would be difficult to apply because of the different economic positions of various firms.

Jordan projected that productivity increases would equal upward wage adjustment if principles were perfectly applied, but experience proved that wages increased more than the cost of living when it rose, and were not reduced as much when it fell. He recommended to Sloan that GM apply tacit rather than government-based automatic wage adjustments because he believed that the formal, open adjustment only invited extended government control over prices and wages, creating more problems than were solved.

New York executives and board members hedged on Wilson's concepts. The war, and its wage and price controls, delayed their introduction, and issues of the postwar 113-day GM-UAW strike—especially the unresolved question of "ability to pay"—busied the company. A desire for some national legislation to control labor extremes and a distrust of UAW Communists also possibly slowed General Motors' introduction of these principles.

The Contribution of Leon Trotsky

From his exile in Mexico, spurned Soviet Communist Leon Trotsky began formulating some of his own ideas about escalation, probably totally unaware of the GM executives' consideration of the concept. The Bolshevik had been second in power during Lenin's rule. After losing out to Stalin in the power struggle following Lenin's 1924 death, Trotsky was expelled from the Communist Party in 1927 and later exiled. The man with the rimless pince-nez, mustache and "Mandrake" beard penned his "Transitional Program for Socialist Revolution" in Mexico in 1938. The program guided the founding conference of the Fourth International and opposed Russia's ongoing Stalinism.

Trotsky's program emphasized that workers must fight and unite around the slogan "a sliding scale of wages," especially as wartime's inflationary pressures increased. Wages should follow price movements, with a strictly guaranteed minimum, or floor, limiting wage declines. (The guaranteed minimum concept would be negotiated into contracts that followed The Bargain.)

Trotsky placed his escalation concept into a markedly different program and purpose than General Motors officials outlined. The socialist coupled escalation with a sliding scale of hours and a division of work among existing workers to assure employment for all. Militant trade unionism and public works were to accompany implementation of his concepts. These were "transitional" demands to Trotsky which would help develop the organized strength of the proletariat for its ultimate dictatorship.

He had little faith in the easy or immediate actualization of these transitional demands. When asked, "Can we actually realize the slogan (a sliding scale of wages and hours)?" he replied, "It is easier to overthrow capitalism than to realize this demand under capitalism." And he went on, "Not one of our demands will be realized under capitalism. That is why we are calling them transitional demands. It creates a bridge to the mentality of the workers and then a material bridge to the socialist revolution."

The exiled former Communist expected resistance to escalation in the United States, especially from "lawyers, property owners and small and ruined capitalists." He predicted bureaucrats would also oppose it, and if it became popular with the masses, fascist tendencies would develop in opposition to it. In order to protect themselves from ruin and to get on with the socialist struggle, he advised workers to fight for escalation.

As he further considered what a sliding scale of wages and hours would mean to workers, he decided that it would go beyond a mere temporary, transitional step, and that it would introduce socialism in a simple, popular way to American workers, who looked upon European socialism as too utopian. When he pondered what a sliding scale of wages and hours actually meant, Trotsky concluded, "In reality it is the system of work in socialist society. The total number of workers divided into the total number of hours."

Trotsky was assassinated in Mexico in 1940, the year before Charles Wilson became president of General Motors. Yet his followers credit his propaganda as a driving force behind UAW workers' eventually "taking up this demand in its negotiations" and "winning" the escalator clause from GM in 1948. Furthermore, they claim that since The Bargain's adoption, bosses have tried to "deny, restrict or withdraw" the escalator clause, while workers tried to "obtain, keep or extend its application." Trotskyites maintain that BLS favors employers, that escalation should co-ordinate with a sliding scale of hours to fight unemployment, and that all workers, organized or unorganized, should benefit from a sliding scale of wages and hours.

Attitudes of UAW Leaders toward Escalation

Union members read about and responded to Trotsky's ideas in *The Militant,* the Socialist Worker Party newspaper. Some members of the United Automobile Workers began advocating escalation as an issue for wage negotiations. Socialist UAW member John Anderson raised the issue with General Motors local officers some time between November, 1940 and May, 1943. In December, 1943, the UAW Executive Board put forward an escalation proposal in their upcoming wage negotiations. Again, before the 1945-46 strike, Socialist Worker Party members advocated a cost-of-living adjustment demand. And in March, 1947, Anderson repeated his demand at the national UAW-GM conference. The opposition of Reutherites and Communists to the Socialist Worker Party proposals aborted them. Opponents often argued that wage escalation might freeze wages at current real levels. The CIO, UAW executive board and policy council and the GM Council all opposed the escalator clause in their 1947-48 formal negotiating sessions.

Just months before the 1948 negotiations began, Walter Reuther squelched a serious effort of five Flint, Michigan local UAW presidents to re-introduce a wage escalation demand. According to some observers, Reuther considered it not just an issue, but a real political challenge.

The five UAW local presidents who advocated escalation represented about fifty thousand workers, did not belong to either Socialist or Communist parties, but they feared the effect of Reuther's power on the union. Francis R. "Jack" Palmer, head of Local 659, led this faction with Joe Berry of Buick Local 599, Bob Carter of A.C. Sparkplug Local 651, Larry Finnan of Fisher Body Local 581 and Bill Connally of Fisher Body Local 598. Originally, Palmer supported Reuther against the Thomas-Addes-Leonard caucus, but now he regretted lack of opposition to Reuther because he believed that internal union competition led to more concessions for the workers. "Any organization. . . after it gets control. . . also gets arthritis," he philosophized.

The five proposed a twenty-five cent hourly wage increase to make up for price increases since the May, 1947 negotiations. They also sought a sliding scale cost-of-living adjustment on wages. The Flint presidents reminded workers that the government predicted that prices would increase 10 to 20 percent in the upcoming three to six months. They called for a quarterly adjustment according to the BLS CPI, and advocated that a wage floor be negotiated.

Palmer ran for UAW president on the Five Presidents' platform and spoke on radio to discuss the demands in January, 1948. At once their ideas received so much solid support that it staggered their imaginations. Ford Local 600, with eighty thousand members, backed them, as did Briggs Local 212. Four smaller Detroit GM unions also joined the grass-roots movement, which won over two hundred thousand supporters. A *Detroit News* labor reporter interpreted the Five Presidents' Program as a hint of Reuther's 1948 wage demands, covertly initiated from central union headquarters. Others considered it an effort to put Reuther in a choiceless position of third round wage leadership.

Reuther was on the spot. He rushed to Flint to speak out against the proposals. The United Automobile Workers had earlier promised to work out wage demands with sister organizations, such as the United Steel Workers. The strategy meetings that were to start the new year in 1948 were impaired by the timing of the five presidents. That twenty-five-cent bid might also undermine larger initial demands union officials probably had prepared. The irate UAW president stated that the proposition went against previous convention rejections. He pointed out that the Oil Workers International Union planned to end their short-term escalation experiment with Sinclair Oil Company because members feared cuts and favored flat increases. Escalation froze worker living standards and might even cut wages. In case prosperity lasted longer for automobile companies than for industry in general, a Bureau of Labor Statistics–based index would prevent automobile workers from sharing in their employers' well-being.

Palmer claimed that Reuther only opposed wage escalation because he wanted to crush political opposition. The people, not the program, were at issue, Palmer noted, and he accused the UAW president of "Redbaiting" them. "Reuther quoted from the Communist Party newspaper, and then from my radio address, and then said, 'These are the people who are trying to destroy our union,' " Palmer recalled.

Reuther undermined the five presidents in order to keep his power secure, and to prevent fragmented leadership at a very crucial time. He also opposed escalation out of legitimate fears expressed by many union members that it would freeze real wages. It was a delicate issue, since Reuther had always tacitly sought to keep wages attuned to cost-of-living increases. He also thought workers deserved continually improving living standards as well as a larger proportion of the national income. He saw no immediate hope in escalation schemes that had been tried or proposed, but he specified his misgivings about them. In doing so, he facilitated future discussion of the very proposal Wilson readied.

5

The Bargain Achieved

THE UNITED AUTOMOBILE WORKERS approached General Motors first in 1948 because it was the largest and richest company. The advancements attained there they could probably gain later from other companies with less effort. The union usually asked GM for wage increases they believed the company would give them to avoid a debilitating strike. Typically GM remained more stubborn about principles, so the UAW generally initiated demands of principles elsewhere.

UAW negotiator Jack Livingston once said about GM bargainers: "They were rough, they were tough, but one good thing about bargaining with GM, you never had to be ashamed to ask for money." GM negotiator Lou Seaton overheard Livingston and wryly commented, "That's right, Jack. We've got it. All you have to do is get it."

Almost a quarter million members looked to thirteen UAW representatives to battle eight GM negotiators for their well-being. The union served an unprecedented 132 demands on GM March 12, 1948, and threatened "the GM titans" to "the damnedest struggle ever." Husky, tough-talking GM labor-relations staff member Lou Seaton considered this the most drastic set of demands ever made on the company, but he recognized certain demands as being more crucial to UAW members.

Negotiations Begin

The negotiators met in Room 5-202 of the General Motors Building, directly across from UAW headquarters. The rooms in those days were furnished with what Seaton remembered as "some of the damnedest old furniture, anything they could find," contrary to their modernized atmosphere today. The men sat in double rows around a small conference table. Whenever necessary, each team could retreat into smaller caucus rooms adjoining the main bargaining room.

Only bland light filtered through venetian blinds into the smoky, hazy room. Lou Seaton remembered he changed from smoking cigarettes to cigars during these negotiations, after he discovered he absentmindedly had three burning cigarettes in the ash tray in front of him. Behind closed doors, negotiators sparred for hours, scratched down notes and doodled. UAW representative Jack Conway proved himself a "prize doodler," judged Seaton, who commented, "We should have had his art work psychoanalyzed to forecast union thinking."

In the caucus rooms, representatives convened privately and made hush-hush phone calls from telephone booths especially installed in caucus rooms to insure privacy. They could drink soft drinks or fruit juice stored in refrigerators, or snack on leftovers they might have saved from free nonalcoholic lunches the company provided for all. Each caucus room had its huge, old-fashioned water cooler topped with a glass water-filled tank. To add a lighter moment to the serious business of negotiation, a union representative put some goldfish in the cooler with the sign, "Please do not gulp our guppies" on it.

The union, which previously fought its battles for wages in the press as well, kept reporters at a distance and dismissed their court reporter. Only the company-assigned stenographer took notes in this session. Lou Seaton remembered that automobile union bargainer Art Johnstone told the company that it now had an opportunity to revive collective bargaining after complaining of too many government directives. Johnstone reminded the group that formerly, only government intervention or labor threats and forces prompted General Motors to live up to its responsibilities. "He saw this negotiation as an opportunity for us to show the world that we could progress without outside intervention, and he told us so," Seaton recalled. Another UAW man, E.J. Patterson, told Seaton at the time that War Labor Board directives imposed upon both parties in the 1945-46 strike produced more than collective bargaining had. Patterson also told Seaton that union men believed collective bargaining now held more promise, that it was a "new era" as far as they saw it.

Each team of negotiators kept its own secrets as it tried to outguess the others. A United Automobile Worker man astonished General Motors conferees when he produced a company bargaining report meant strictly for top executives. Later they traced the leak to a GM mimeograph operator who dated a UAW public-relations man.

Deliberate privacy and a renewed sense of their importance drew these men closer together than ever before over their differences. "It's just you and me now," was the attitude among these veterans of 1930's bitter strife and the 1940's government-tempered contests. President Walter Reuther, who stood on a factory platform to begin a sit-down strike in the 1930's, politely sat down at the bargaining table for forty days of negotiations before an assailant shot him. Thomas Arthur "Art" Johnstone and John W. "Jack" Livingston took over for Reuther and consulted him at the hospital and at his home, just as company representatives kept Wilson informed in his upstairs office in the General Motors building.

For the UAW

Art Johnstone knew what hard labor meant. As a thirteen-year-old "hired man" he plowed fields with eight horses in tandem to earn a living. He emigrated to Detroit from Canada, and in 1928, Pontiac Motors Car Company hired him as a dock loader for fifty cents an hour. Regular eleven hour days stretched into fifteen and sixteen hour days without the premium overtime pay. When he tried to organize fellow dock loaders to seek more just work practices, his supervisor dismissed him. Shortly afterwards, concealing his previous employment, he got a job framing coaches for Yellow Truck and Coach Company, the General Motors Truck and Coach Division. Johnstone became one of the first UAW members and he directed their General Motors department in 1948.

Jack Livingston resigned from the presidency of his local union at St. Louis' Ford assembly plant to join the UAW International staff in 1939. In those early organizing days, Pinkerton detectives trailed him. He discovered this when National Labor Relations Board workers asked him if he had been to certain places on certain days. He asked them how they knew so much. They revealed they confiscated Pinkerton Detective Agency records. In 1948 as UAW-CIO president, he attended his ninth bargaining session. In Lou Seaton's judgment, Livingston was the "top man" and Johnstone the "articulate fellow."

For GM

Seaton, who did most of the talking for General Motors in this session, also knew the working world. A Detroit chart-and-poster firm hired him as their messenger boy when he was in the eighth grade. He attended Wayne University several years before Victor and Walter Reuther enrolled there. Seaton joined General Motors' sales section in 1928, then moved to industrial relations four years later. His casual grammar, wit and dockworker expletives enlivened negotiations for the next thirty years.

GM's vice president in charge of personnel, Harry Anderson, negotiated less than Seaton, but in 1948 he was the company's "top man at the table." Management and labor leaders alike knew him as a quiet but determined negotiator. His dignified manner, accented by a bow tie, gave him a professorial air. Anderson came to GM labor relations in the 1930's after receiving legal training at Detroit College of Law and holding sales positions in GM and other companies. He often assisted "C.E." Wilson. (In 1959, his life ended tragically when retired GM president Harlow Curtice shot him in a duck-hunting accident.)

Seaton expected a "labor show" the first week: the union "would pound the table and tell GM what bums they were, getting personal grievances from the plants off their chests." The UAW accused GM of disrupting union loyalty with the company group-insurance program. Union officials thought they could win a jointly-administered employer-financed group-insurance policy. GM reminded them that the National Labor Relations Act validated collective bargaining only on wage, hour and working condition questions. Labor men insisted that benefits be made "conditions of employment" but the NLRB suspended the question during negotiations, pending decisions on two cases. As far as loyalty was concerned, General Motors representatives noted it was "not an either/or proposition." A worker could maintain several loyalties: family, church, political party, country, company and union.

News reporters played up the perennial union shop demand in these negotiations. The UAW still had a wartime maintenance-of-membership clause which said not every worker had to join a union, but those who did must remain. It was reported that Johnstone said General Motors' refusal of a union shop demonstrated its desire to restrict and contain the union. Seaton remembered Johnstone saying that a union became fully useful and carried out contract obligations under union shop provisions, which signalled complete acceptance of a union as a constructive force. But Seaton claimed: ". . . If you take a fair look at the relationship down through the years, you will find that rather than the corporation's unwillingness or failure to accept the union, it has been an unwillingness on the part of the union to accept the corporation." Johnstone called Seaton's statement "absurd" and challenged him to a debate. "We will probably document it before we finish," Seaton responded, and the argument got lost in more concrete issues.

Negotiations Proceed

The plodding, enervating discussion over these issues led to the ultimate question of how much money General Motors would add to wages and perhaps also to product prices. "A monstrous monument to unbridled greed," were the words the UAW officials used to deride General Motors' 1948 first quarter profits. Profits approached 28 percent on investment, were six times wartime norms, and the greatest ever accumulated in a single three-month period by any corporation. Automobile union researchers informed General Motors what they would do if they had such profits to divide: "Cut the retail price of passenger cars by $130 each, raise factory worker wages fifty cents an hour, give equivalent percentage increases to salaried workers and still maintain profits of 6 percent on stockholders' investment."

Seaton described their argument as "just a propaganda ploy for the great, unwashed American public." Because they considered the company profitable, the union wanted to interject "ability to pay," but Seaton argued that after General Motors paid necessary expenses, profits were lower relative to national income than they had been in any previous year because business had run at high volumes but sold at "perilously narrow profit margins." In addition, General Motors needed more capital to produce the same amount of goods. In order to meet market needs, General Motors as well as other companies had made heavy commitments for new plants and equipment. Bond issues, bank loans and drawing on cash accounts resulted. Recession might weigh heavily on such action by business. Limiting profits to the degree union men desired would prohibit industrial expansion, the company countered. Researchers manipulated figures unaccountably, and General Motors accused union statisticians of relating total profit on all operations (half of which consisted of nonpassenger car manufacture) to passenger-car production only. This made profits per unit appear twice as high as they actually were. GM also said that union men underestimated increased labor costs by about half, because they did not account for half the total work done by persons in supplying and extractive industries who would require wage increases comparable to GM employees.

They might just as easily have said GM could give away all its green Cadillac convertibles and still enjoy a profit. General Motors assured them that these convertibles represented only a small fraction of a percent of company output. Seaton warned that ability-to-pay arguments, when couched in a union tirade against company profits and executive bonuses, gained little favor. He suggested they change their focus from company ability to pay to the merits of a wage increase.

By March 23, the United Automobile Workers reduced its initial $1.44 demand to forty-five cents, and began stressing cost-of-living anxieties. Part of their concern stemmed from the fact that workers no longer had wartime overtime pay to help them maintain their living standards. They wanted twenty-five cents just to catch up with their loss in real earnings since June, 1946, and wanted to project future living-cost increases into the wage settlement.

Using the Bureau of Labor Statistics study of the budget of a Detroit worker's family, it was estimated that an annual salary of $3,293 provided minimum subsistence for a family of four. UAW men charged that GM workers in 1947 averaged $290 less than this standard. The union men added that the BLS basis was no better than the 1934-35 relief budget in accounting for decent worker-living standards.

General Motors statisticians countered that, according

to a postwar survey of company employees based on withholding tax certificates, the size of the average GM worker's family was 2.7 persons, including the head of the household, and that a budget for four was excessive. The BLS in 1947 estimated that a typical city family of three could live adequately on an annual salary of $2756. General Motors factory workers in the cities studied averaged $272 above that figure. The dignity of reasoned debate strained under this daily stress of figure fights.

At least workers needed to keep up with living costs. Automobile Union research director Nat Weinberg forecast that by May 15, the Consumer Price Index would reach 175, based on the 1935-39 index. Seaton and Johnstone literally gambled on the cost-of-living index. Seaton wagered it would stand closer to 165 than to Johnstone's 175 by May 15. Their stakes were malted milk shakes at Shapero's Drug store on the first floor of the GM Building. By mid-May the index was so close to 170 as to defy a milk shake, and probably merited dutch treat on more potent beverages. Weinberg protested that the food and farm product declines influenced the lower figures more than he predicted, and he declared his timing wrong. Instead, the index would reach 175 by August or September, he argued.

Dissension and debate centered around how to measure changing living standards. Seaton told deliberators that he was "thinking seriously" about bringing a series of charts to the table. These would use arbitrary Consumer Price Index starting points from around 1919, and would prove that either side could make a good case for itself depending upon the selected starting point. The union called this choosing of their best base "the reflection of perspective." The economics department of General Motors made a slide rule for Seaton to show the Consumer Price Index as far back as 1890, and by operating it, Seaton could discern projected wage increases, and "keep up with Nat Weinberg's arguments."

UAW negotiators insisted that workers deserved a

raise in real wages because they contributed to American productivity. They said that workers as well as capital expenses bettered productivity, and that capital accumulation tended to deprive workers of their just recompense. American mass production required continuing pay increases in order that the workers might be good consumers, the union claimed.

"Lou, you know we came in here with our empty basket and we've been here almost two months now, and I looked in my basket the other day and there wasn't anything in it," Johnstone told Seaton. Seaton replied, "That's right, Art, and there isn't going to be anything in it for a while until the time is right."

Influence of Other Negotiations

Management in other heavy goods industries resisted wage demands, and GM and the UAW kept wary watch over them. On April 18, Chrysler offered workers a six-cent wage hike, but UAW negotiators held out for their initial thirty-five cent demand. Seventy-five thousand workers struck Chrysler plants. Five days later GM laid off two hundred thousand metal-fabricating workers for ten days because earlier coal strikes caused pig iron and steel shortages. Ford officials rejected the Automobile Union's thirty-cent hourly wage bid, and told workers they might reduce average hourly wages.

General Electric Company refused to increase United Electrical Worker pay while United States Steel Company turned down their workers' requests for increases. Some 80,000 United Packinghouse Workers accepted a nine-cent wage increase after they dropped their demand for 29 cents. They lost an estimated $40 million in wages because they could have settled for nine cents before the strike.

Back in Room 5-202, Seaton told negotiators not to expect to be able to announce a General Motors offer at the April United Automobile Workers meeting. "I understand you will give away two automobiles, so you have a purpose for the meeting," Seaton joked at the time. Johnstone answered seriously that they did not hold the meeting to give away automobiles. At the meeting, two hundred union representatives from General Motors plants met to ask local unions to complete strike polls of their members by May 23, as the strike deadlines was May 28.

Congress of Industrial Organizations officials warned of inevitable strikes in either automobile or electric industries, and sought substantial wage settlements to sustain their 1948 wage drive. GM men believed that "under Walter Reuther's genius," the union believed in "taking on one at a time," and would not strike GM while they struck Chrysler. Without a Chrysler settlement or an acceptable GM offer, the UAW could avoid or delay walkouts only if they extended the previous contract or agreed to work without one. UAW officials discussed neither of these possibilities. If GM offered nothing or something unacceptable, the UAW would have to strike or they would undermine their threats in future negotiations. Johnstone noticed a lack of militance among workers, but thought that regardless of their unpreparedness, they would disrupt production if automobile workers' negotiators "went home with an empty basket." For agonizing days Wilson did not give Seaton anything to fill the union basket. Other than the eventual 1948 offer, he prepared no alternate proposals.

Tensions Heighten

On May 18, the United Automobile Workers filed a ten-day intent-to-strike General Motors notice at the Michigan labor mediation board office. UAW negotiator Jack Conway informed Seaton in their May 23rd session that "the steam valve must be screwed down or up tomorrow night." Seaton thought that was a reminder to him that if they built up for work stoppage, they could not turn it off like a light switch, but must either get results or have a period of time to cool down. About ninety plants voted to strike on Friday, May 28, while five key plants rejected the proposed action.

Wilson's GM associates in New York City held a finance committee meeting, required by company rules because Wilson's proposal meant the corporation would spend over a million dollars. Mixed feelings emerged in debates about introducing wage escalation and productivity factoring in the 1948 agreement, thus promoting their adoption in nationwide wage policies. Some executives remarked, "Keep it a short-run mechanism for GM. If it works for a while, we've had that much peace. If it blows up, we carry on from there."

Others saw it as a sound, long-run policy for GM only. Still others considered it good for the country as well as GM. The finance committee decided that the company should advocate wage escalation and productivity for itself, continue as long as possible, and if GM set an example which other industries followed—fine.

Formal Introduction of Cost-of-living Allowances

On May 21, Seaton descended from a conference with Wilson, and resolved the following aims to the restless men in Room 5-202: To re-establish the buying power of an hour of work during and since the war on a sound basis; to protect the buying power of an hour of work by making cost of living adjustments periodically; to improve the buying power of an hour of work to insure the worker an improved standard of living; and to stabilize labor-management relations over a longer period of time. Union and company negotiators decided to choose eight men from among them, discuss ideas then make a settlement. They also agreed to abstain from comments to the press, except for issuing a joint statement to announce final failure or success.

Making press secrecy imperative yet difficult was the fact that GM and the United Electrical Workers were stalemated at a similar stage of negotiations previous to the announcement of the General Motors proposal. GM told automobile union men they planned to issue similar proposals "in the future" to the UE and the other eighteen international unions the company dealt with but they wanted to present the principles first to the UAW because it represented the largest group of employees.

General Motors negotiator Earl Bramblett saw "intrigued and fascinated faces" across the table when Seaton presented the proposal. Nothing had hinted of the introduction of such innovations, yet to some union negotiators it seemed a suitable response to documents and wage demands they had presented. Seaton thought Johnstone called it "an impressive statement," but because it was general, it would require much elaboration. He went on to ask for an immediate "preliminary exploration" but Seaton thought it unwise to spend the rest of the afternoon sketching over such complex ideas. Besides, he told them, they wanted to "check some figure work" in order to be "damn sure of the material" they set up. The United Automobile Workers men spent much of that night in one of their homes speculating upon how many cents per hour such a settlement might yield. Someone left a window open and Art Johnstone caught a terrible cold.

The eight chosen negotiators, in "small committee," discussed whether the increment in the cost of living would produce another penny per hour in wages, and to what base year to refer in calculating living-cost increases. The parties agreed upon 1935-39 as their reference base, as it was the last period in which prices had been fairly stable. Price changes had not been major factors in wage adjustment. The sides also discussed other reference bases which would have favored labor (higher wage increases) or management (lower wage increases) more than the base selected.

From the 1935-39 reference base, they determined that consumer prices had increased approximately 69 percent. GM workers had in that interim received only about a 60 percent increase in their average wage. GM compensated them 9 percent of their average wage in the base period, or eight cents an hour in cost-of-living adjustment pay (COLAs). To determine whether the increase in the cost of living would illicit another penny per hour, the negotiators calculated as follows: they decided to keep the relationship between the prevailing average hourly wage in April 1948, which was $1.49, and the latest available consumer price index figure of 169.3 (1935-1939 = 100, or a 69.3 per cent cost-of-living increase since the base year). Negotiators divided the average wage of $1.49 into the index figure of 169.3, and agreed upon a one-cent increase for ever 1.14 points movement in the price index.

To calculate the annual improvement factor, they took 2 percent of the average wage of $1.49, which amounted to almost three cents per hour, and UAW officials identified it as a three-cent increase meant to improve worker living standards, rather than a 2 percent productivity increase. They presented it as a three-cent pay raise because they believed workers would have a more positive response than if it had been presented as an incentive and a reward for increased productivity.

In retrospect, Art Johnstone recalled, "GM originally proposed a three cents per hour addition to the base rate; I demurred and shoved a slip of paper across the table on which was written, 'Chrysler 6¢, me, too.' " He believed the United Automobile Workers needed at least a solid, dependable six-cent increase, which had been Chrysler's original offer. A General Motors man responded, "That's OK, Art, we can fix that." Six cents of the wage increase was made permanent, regardless of the BLS index—three cents from the annual improvement factor; three cents of the eight-cent cost-of-living increase.

"I almost got fired over this," Seaton laughed. "I moved the three cents of the cost of living to an immovable wage increase. It didn't cost us any more because we were going to give eight cents to keep the cost of living up, but now only five cents of that eight cents would be subject to reduction.

"I went upstairs and explained to Mr. Wilson that I destroyed the pure concept of his theory that he had already sold to the board of directors when I froze the three cents. He was a little put out and had to do some phoning. It defeated the principle in Mr. Wilson's eyes, but he wasn't dissatisfied with the final product. He recognized the practical aspects of it. In fact, he even dressed up the wording of the contract."

General Motors wanted a three-year contract, but settled for the union limit of two years, with possible future longer-term agreements. The United Automobile Workers worried about maintaining member loyalties and solid organization over a three-year period, but they were willing to try a two-year agreement.

False Alarm

The public press spread a strike alarm a week before contract deadline. Governor Kim Sigler of Michigan summoned negotiator Harry Anderson to meet him at Detroit's Cadillac Square Building.

At the meeting, Sigler offered federal mediation, but Anderson turned him down. If mediators stepped in at that late date (May 21), both sides would have to "put on their whole show from the start," Anderson explained. He added that the parties could "see the lighthouse" in small committee and told the governor of their progress off the record. Reporters interpreted Anderson's visit to Sigler as a basis for optimism regarding quick settlement, and rumors of a six- to ten-cent hourly wage offer spread. Company spokesmen had no comment.

Near the Anderson-Sigler meeting place at the Book-Cadillac Hotel, UAW executive board members met on May 27 and 28 to review contract proposals. Earlier, they met in Reuther's home and discussed provisions with the UAW president who had just returned from the hospital. Reuther noticed nothing "magic" about the formula. He thought GM predetermined that they wished an eleven-cent increase, then designed the formula to comply. They chose straight time average wages of $1.50, which included all fringe adjustments except shift premium, which UAW officials called an inflated figure. In spite of some objections, they agreed to accept the contract for its principles.

Livingston remembered that the concepts made sense to them. "If the cost of living went down, our improvement factor still worked and people's cost of living went down. Then if the cost of living went up, we were still in a better position than ever to argue for more on the improvement factor." He further reflected, "Had we been making just a straight wage settlement, we might have insisted very vigorously on even more at the time, but we were very much in agreement with the basic principle." Other union demands during this session vanished.

On May 25, at 6:30 A.M., typists on the eleventh floor of the General Motors Building finished the contract. After twenty hours of continuous bargaining in the thirty-seventh session, negotiators released copies of their agreement to the reporters, who had been awakened and summoned at 4:00 A.M.

Announcement of The Bargain

General Motors' public relations staff held a rushed seminar for reporters laboring under a deadline, with a public-relations man assigned to help each reporter. They had to explain what the eleven-cent cost increase meant: eight cents to adjust for the cost of living, three cents of which could be eliminated and three cents a solid productivity-based increase to assure improved living standards during each year of the two-year contract. Veteran Detroit labor reporter Jack Crellin said they were accustomed to hearing about nickel and dime increases and he couldn't get the difference straight between cost-of-living allowances and annual-improvement factors. "I think

General Motors did an excellent job of educating us in the long run, but for several hours, we were still baffled," Crellin remembered.

"The only guy who really understood it was Stan Brams," Lou Seaton judged. Brams was publisher of *Labor Trends*, and Detroit editorial manager of McGraw-Hill publications (including *Business Week*). He noted at the time that the UAW never contradicted the way GM heralded the contract concepts as Wilson's great development. "Here was a logical, simple, dramatic story. This man is sick and thinking about what he can do to solve problems and he comes up with a brand new formula," Brams said. He noticed that people responded with "here is a formula that will insure labor peace for generations."

General Motors expected to spend $75 million a year for wages, while gaining two years of uninterrupted production. Some automakers predicted auto price increases, but Wilson said not at least until 1949 models came out. The longer-term contract gave GM more assurance that it could meet its long-range production schedules. GM offered forty thousand United Electrical Workers on their payroll the same agreement and they accepted it. A week later, GM gave one hundred thousand salaried employees four percent COLA increases and promised to adjust salaries quarterly.

UAW members were sent to locals throughout the United States and Canada to explain the contract to workers. They found their task difficult because workers were just used to more pay in their envelopes and this was a complex formula tied to living-cost figures. They told workers the contract meant $55 million a year in increased purchasing power for them, and GM would be able to absorb it without dunning consumers with higher prices. They deliberately reminded workers not to happily anticipate price increases. Local unions took a majority vote determination of their membership which a majority of their local-appointed delegates approved on June 7, 1948. Victor Reuther assessed that when workers lived with the agreement and enjoyed its benefits, they would understand it better.

The two men, Wilson and Reuther, who probably did the most to bring about the contract, did not sign it. Shortly after the ink dried, they attended a luncheon meeting in Detroit of the Mayor's Labor-Management-Citizens' Committee at which Wilson told of his hospital legend and reminded prominent persons present that he, a trained engineer, liked to use principles to minimize disagreement.

"It wasn't difficult to come up with the idea of the cost of living clause, because others had used it before," Wilson said. "I didn't believe employees of General Motors, who hadn't created inflation, ought to be adversely affected by it any more than could be avoided."

He continued, "I would say that the annual improvement factor was more decidedly original with us, as far as I know. If General Motors can't meet the nation's average improvement in productivity, then we're incompetent as a management."

Walter Reuther sat back in his chair and let Wilson rejoice over what everyone considered "Wilson's Baby." Born of the thought of many men, and bred by a more legitimized labor-management "shotgun marriage," the new formula always needed further explanation.

6

Trial by Era

"WE THINK WE HAVE STARTED something new," Harry Anderson proclaimed as negotiators signed the new contract. "It was a settlement reached by good, old-fashioned collective bargaining." This "something old, something new, something borrowed" Bargain surely would last. Confident bleary-eyed negotiators recommended it to other unions, but not everyone agreed and followed.

Mixed Reviews

Walter Reuther and Jack Livingston rushed to Congress of Industrial Organizations national president Philip Murray in Pittsburgh to herald the contract. At the time, Murray's Steelworkers were locked into a no-strike contract and he worried that they might miss advantages other workers received, but he approved of the concepts. John L. Lewis and others spurned the unorthodox wage settlement because they preferred a large and healthy cash settlement rather than annual improvement factor (AIF) and COLA driblets. They looked upon The Bargain as "the negotiating of a boy scout," commented Victor Reuther.

Rank-and-file members questioned, "How can the leadership claim eleven cents as a victory after telling us the minimum we needed was thirty cents and we get an escalator besides?"

Communists accused GM of dividing the labor unions and preventing their close-knit struggle, while industrialists admonished the giant automobile company for ending "no third-round pay increases" unity among businessmen. Contrary to newspaper columnist Drew Pearson's rumors that "the big boys of industry" at their "Waldorf Conference" decided to contain wages between nine and eleven cents, other key automakers claimed that GM's sudden settlement caught them off guard, in a state of "shocked chagrin." Neither Ford nor Chrysler really approved of the General Motors action.

Wilson ironically used time he won from longer-term contracts to defend his ideas in speeches, public statements and private meetings. He discussed the contract over luncheon one day with Frank Rising, one of few automotive people bold enough to openly challenge the new GM agreement. Rising, a former labor editor of *Business Week*, at the time headed the Automotive Parts Association, representing 400 GM suppliers.

"If you use this automatic cost-of-living increase widely," he argued with Wilson, "you will find that raising the price of labor raises the price of goods, which raises the cost of living, which raises the price of labor. . . like a dog chasing its own tail."

Wilson then admitted that Rising had reason for lack of enthusiasm but countered that the GM plan relieved both sides of much wrangling and would regularize labor relations. He also believed that the reassured workers would stay with GM, and work harder for promotions because of the contract.

To answer the accusation that The Bargain was inflationary, Wilson consistently argued that it was neither inflationary nor deflationary, but merely followed price movements. Wilson countered that wars, strikes, crop failures, dislocating government financial and tax policies, and bank credit policies could be inflationary. Workers and executives could exercise little influence over these causes of inflation, Wilson believed, and workers should be compensated for losses due to the inflation they did not cause.

Later, Wilson discovered that smaller auto-parts companies raised wages more than the large auto companies between 1940 and 1950. He thought small businesses as well as large might adopt a similar contract, and would be capable of paying the wages if every company improved methods to enhance output per worker. The GM president hoped others would turn away from "shotgun bargaining" and apply the principles, not necessarily the monetary terms of this new agreement. Reuther recognized that many companies could not meet these terms, and suggested in this and subsequent years that they trim contracts to suit particular bargaining situations. In the first years following the contract, few companies adopted it, but many felt its impact. Others had to be convinced that it would last, weather criticism, overcome unforeseen flaws and live up to its grandiose promise. The Bargain was on trial.

In Retrospect

In the first two years of the contract, GM accrued the lowest time lost to work stoppages in its history. When cost-of-living decreases justified wage cuts, UAW representatives visited local unions to reaffirm the validity of the agreement and Reuther's authority to uphold it. The ability to enforce The Bargain was closely related to Reuther's power position in the union as well as his good faith in keeping the agreement. GM noticed little union resentment over wage cuts according to the formula. At the same time, the company reduced its car prices fifteen dollars for every one-point decrease in the CPI. The company reinvested its profits considerably, and credited its best operations ever to a combination of postwar consumer demand and labor peace. By 1950, other manufacturers had adopted the long-term aspect of The Bargain. The wage-escalation concept was to become more popular and to prove its value to workers during the inflationary Korean War.

By 1950, both GM and the UAW recognized that The Bargain had passed its initial test. Its renewal, amplification and extension was announced in a headline in a Detroit newspaper: "Five Years of Industrial Peace." If the event was now given more dramatic play in the press, it might have been because reporters understood it better and grasped the implications more clearly. Management and labor were perhaps more sure of themselves now, and encouraged the publicity more.

The labor peace hinted at in that historic 1948 Bargain was now magnified by its 1950 extension. The renewed contract carried air-tight assurances against strikes for five years because the union had agreed to seek no contract changes for five years. National Labor Relations Board spokesmen pointed out that if labor failed to live up to its 1950 commitments, GM could charge the UAW before the NLRB with breech of contract or bad-faith bargaining.

The cost-of-living wage adjustment, with its protective floor beneath wages, continued in 1950. The annual improvement factor was increased from three to four cents (from 2 percent, to 2.5 percent of average worker wages). Additionally, those who reached 65 years of age with at least twenty-five years of GM service would receive pensions of $100 monthly, including social security payments. Insurance benefits were increased at no added expense to workers.

The union and the company met halfway on the union shop question. They agreed that after ninety days a new employee was obligated to join the union as a dues-paying member for one year, after which time he could quit or continue his membership. It was assumed by the union that most workers would stay in after initial recruitment. The UAW had now won the security and prestige it needed to make the longer-term five-year contract more workable.

In 1950, the negotiators had contemplated using an

escape clause that would free both parties from the wage indexation formula if war occurred. But, they decided, escalation suited both wartime and peacetime economies. In 1950, Communists accused GM of signing the contract with an eye for high-speed, high-profit and no-strike war production.

The Bargain survived and even thrived during the Korean War, which generated more spendable income as consumer goods dwindled and inflation increased. The Council of Economic Advisers suggested wage freezes, deferred wage payments and higher taxes. Walter Reuther pleaded with Wage Stabilization Board members not to interfere with cost-of-living adjustments which would "ruin the greatest degree of industrial stability ever in mass-production industry." Because of dwindling supply of labor during the Korean War, industries quickly adopted wage escalation to retain workers who preferred supply of labor escalation to wage-price control.

In March, 1951, the Wage Stabilization Board approved escalation in most previous contracts but said future contracts must limit cost-of-living increases to 10 percent. People complained so much of "leapfrogging" (the WSB's passing of special cases exceeding general regulations), that by summer the board allowed most cost-of-living allowances to keep up with living-cost increases. To critics who said WSB policy was more like controlled inflation than cost-of-living stability, Economic Stabilization administrator Eric Johnston retaliated by stating that government policy merely approved, not insisted upon, business-labor decisions to raise wages.

"Escalation must not be as bad as critics claimed," said Wilson, "if our government adopted it nationwide." He used the same argument to defend one-half percent increases in annual improvement factors, overriding his original 12-percent limit. Steel executives disagreed. They pointed out that inflation resulted during wartime labor shortages, when companies felt compelled to use annual improvement factors even though productivity did not pay for them. Others added that productivity actually decreased in war while plants retooled and new workers were trained. Even the National Association of Manufacturers (its biggest duespayer was GM) called productivity wage increases inflationary.

The WSB accepted GM's (and other) productivity-based increases, as long as companies showed improved output per man hour without raising prices. President Truman and his Council of Economic Advisors approved 3-percent productivity increases but refused CIO claims of 4 percent and American Federation of Labor advocacy of a catch-up productivity raise of 11 percent since 1951.

The Bargain held its basic shape throughout the war until new challenges stretched its limits. Wilson asserted that the UAW would sustain the 1950 five-year contract including a special clause nullifying an NLRB rule that unsettled collective bargaining matters remained negotiable at any time. To Wilson, Reuther seemed far more reliable than former United Automobile Workers leaders.

In July, 1952, steelworkers won a twenty-one-cent flat wage increase. Automobile workers rankled. If they could not reopen their contract until May, 1955, they might lose as much as twenty-five cents of their cost of living increases with a recurrence of the 1949 recession level after the war.

In September of 1952, Reuther announced that the 1950 contract was a "living document," subject to change whenever parties faced drastically new circumstances as they now did. He asked General Motors to secure twenty-one cents of the cost-of-living allowance into a permanent base rate, never subject to reduction even if living costs decreased. He also called for higher annual improvement factors and pensions.

Revision of Cost-of-Living Index by BLS

At the same time, Bureau of Labor Statistics officials revised the index on which the 1950 contract rested. They gave guidance to industry for changing over to the new index by December, 1952. Reuther ordered local unions to ignore these Bureau of Labor Statistics instructions until they examined other settlements. He further vowed to annul the old contract unless he won desired modifications.

Automobile executives were anxious to avoid a breach of contract. They implored government officials to continue publication of the old Bureau of Labor Statistics index, which President Eisenhower authorized to extend through the spring.

UAW-GM negotiations continued intermittently. Reuther refused easy transition to the new index as well as use of the old one because he sought gains from the beginning of the new negotiations. Internal union politics prodded him further. His enemy, Carl Stellato, from the United Automobile Workers' largest local, Ford Local 600, resolved loudly that all future contracts should last only one year. The United Automobile Workers-Congress of Industrial Organizations president countered that at convention, delegates would reconsider long-term contracts. Although many delegates opposed five-year contracts they did not rally around Stellato's one-year-only banner.

Reuther's deliberate impasse backfired. In the third quarter of 1952, cost-of-living adjustment continued to be on the old index. Food costs decreased, and because the old index gave more weight to food costs, the Consumer Price Index dipped from 239.1 to 234.1, causing a one-cent hourly wage cut. The new index presented a slight raise in living costs from 190.8 to 190.9. Use of these figures would have maintained wages.

Problems with CPI

On May 22, 1953, a GM-UAW supplemental agreement gave workers cost of living allowances based on the new BLS index, locking in nineteen of the previous twenty-four-cent gains into the basic wage structure.

Thereafter, the UAW contracted every three years. The new pattern compromised principles and promises but kept the industry stable and fostered prosperity.

The BLS accounted for new spending patterns in revised indices which became controversial in 1952. Labor and management each challenged the use of the index, how to formulate it, and how to keep it objective.

The Consumer Price Index, having gained the spotlight for its increased usefulness, was accused of both understating and overstating price changes. As the complexities of accurately measuring real cost-of-living changes became apparent, it became obvious that a consumer price index could at best only approximate cost-of-living changes.

Observers noticed that the CPI did not account for changes in expenditure patterns during the ten-year period in which the index base and market basket composition remained consistent. If, for example, meat prices increased and consumers substituted chicken for beef, the price index would go up because of the meat price increases, even if consumers spent about the same amount on food with chicken substituted for beef.

A similar distortion occurred as innovations changed people's buying habits. . . for example, when television was introduced. Because of limited supplies, television sets were more expensive at first. As mass markets developed and the economies of scale made television sets cheaper to produce, prices decreased. When the Bureau of Labor Statistics includes such products in the index early in their history, the prices and the index subsequently decline. If the BLS waits until a new product becomes part of the typical consumer spending pattern, the significant decline in prices does not show in the CPI. Under delayed introduction, the CPI tends to either overstate general increases in the price or understate the magnitude of decreases in price. Ewan Clague, BLS Commissioner from 1946-1954, observes that in the compilation of the index, there is a limitation of the sample of priced items to ones that consumers show a continued interest in purchasing. Establishing consumer buying habits takes time, and the necessary delay in registering the item in the index can lead to unavoidable distortions. The decrease in prices of products available at discount outlets also was not quickly recognized and registered in the price index, possibly contributing to this distortion.

The CPI has been faulted for not reflecting quality change. Critics charge that an index that purports to measure cost-of-living changes must be adjusted when manufacturers improve their product or make it more efficient (e.g., automobile engines); when innovations make product maintenance cheaper (e.g., permanent-press shirts); or when lower-cost substitutes are introduced (e.g., compact cars).

Upward biases tend to be balanced by downward biases. For example, the downward bias shows when beef prices decrease, and consumers buy abnormal quantities after having to eat chicken as a lower priced substitute. Similar action occurs when product quality deteriorates or quality of service at outlets decreases, even when prices decrease. As former BLS commissioner Clague stated, "indications are that the procedures which have been followed in the CPI do not involve biases systematically in either direction."

Those who have studied the Consumer Price Index as a measure of cost-of-living changes believe that it is not practical to calculate a monthly price index which adjusts for shifts in consumer expenditure patterns due to price changes (lower-priced chicken substitution for high-priced beef). They believe that the CPI effectively approximates cost of living changes, and might be improved merely by more frequent adjustment of the market basket and base rate, rather than creating a complex cost-of-living index that would adjust for all distortions all the time.

Because the index was regularly revised, it continued to maintain its usefulness in labor relations. It influenced GM and the UAW to agree that no subsequent index revision would affect COLA payments until a new contract dictated it. In addition, both management and labor understood that no retroactive payments would be called for when an index was revised within the term of an agreement.

The first concern that General Motors and the United Automobile Workers showed over Bureau of Labor Statistics figures arose in 1949, when they claimed that the index did not immediately account for higher priced, new dwellings. In August of that year the company arbitrarily added .8 points to the index to avoid reopening the 1948 contract.

When the Korean War sent prices soaring, the Bureau issued an "interim index," which recognized that the more prosperous 1950 consumer spent less of his income on subsistence items. Food expenses were weighted 10 percent lower than formerly, but medical, automobile and miscellaneous expenses were increased by the same percentage.

The revised 1952 Consumer Price Index, on which the 1953 contract was based, also accounted for changes. For the new version, government officials priced 300 items instead of 225, and they studied spending habits of thousands of urban families with $4,000 to $6,000 yearly incomes in forty-six small, medium and large cities. Formerly, the index had been based on families with $3,000 to $5,000 dollars annual income in thirty-four large cities. Surveyors found that housewives bought more newly improved items in the 1949-52 period, in comparison with the previous 1935-39 base period. They now used more margarine, mechanical refrigerators and synthetic detergents than the butter, iceboxes and soap of bygone days. The new version included home ownership and maintenance costs while the old index stressed rental costs. Nylons replaced silk stockings, and restaurant meals, used cars, television sets, beer and babysitters were added.

The Bureau of Labor Statistics computed that the same percentage change in living costs that made the old index move 1.14 points would move the revised index only .68 points. The same slower movement applied to decreases. GM and the UAW agreed upon a principle to make the changeover: approximately a 1-percent hourly pay change for each 1-percent CPI change. For every six-tenths of a point increase in the new index, GM gave an increase of one cent in the hourly wage.

In 1964, the BLS index revision appeared in time for a scheduled GM-UAW contract reconsideration. BLS experts now priced 400 items, and accounted for more new than used cars, more private than public transportation, and more highly processed and frozen foods. The index also reflected credit as well as cash purchases. Because of new living and shopping patterns, the government survey was extended to include suburban areas. The BLS formerly studied families of urban workers and lower-salaried clerical workers. In 1964 the agency computed a second index for families and for single workers. The family index ended in November, 1964, when BLS officials observed that both indices moved in the same patterns. The survey, although limited in funding, expanded to study consumers in fifty-six medium-sized cities. No longer did agency officials account for men's and women's nightwear, appendectomies, sewing machines or lemons in their survey. They added the modern day spending on between-meal-snacks, parking fees, garbage disposals, air conditioners, moving expenses, college tuition, funeral service costs, and federal, state, city and property taxes. Auto and property taxes were likewise included in BLS accounting. However, income, personal property and Social Security taxes were not included.

A revised 1971 CPI index changed the reference base from the period 1957-59 to the year 1967. It surveyed 4,900 urban wage earners and clerical workers with an average family income of $6,250 yearly. In spring of 1978, a revised index extended the index base to include the urban families, professional workers, other white collar workers as well as the unemployed, reflecting far more accurately the range of CPI wage escalation.

Both labor and management kept a close and watchful eye on the Consumer Price Index. (When the bureau made an error in computation in 1974, GM paid its workers an extra cent per hour in cost-of-living wages.) The CPI recorded price changes, accounted for buying habits, expanded to consider more varied consumers and incorporated higher living standards. Its flexibility disconcerted some. Earl Bramblett thought, "it was amazing how many times the CPI increased exactly enough to require a pay increase." Once the New York subway fare rose just enough to advance wages, even though few General Motors workers used the transportation system. Another time, a Florida frost pushed up the cost of oranges, augmenting COLAs. In spite of occasional doubts about the index, both sides expressed satisfaction with it, and so it sustained many contracts.

Labor and management co-operated, independent of the BLS, to reshape the original Bargain. GM executives became aware, soon after 1948, that flat COLA and AIF increases based on a percentage of an average worker's wage tended to pull wage rates toward the average over an extended period of time. This equalizing tendency disturbed the traditional difference between the wages of the skilled trades and less-skilled workers. In other words, the 2 percent of the *average* worker wage, or three cent annual improvement factors, amounted to a greater percentage increase in wages for a floor sweeper than for a tool-and-die maker.

Both labor and management recognized this discrepancy and tried to remedy it to avoid controversy. In 1953 and other subsequent years, skilled workers received special increases. In 1955, GM and the UAW changed the previous application of a productivity percentage to an average hourly wage. They began instead to apply their agreed-upon productivity percentage in terms of a scale considering specific wage brackets. As a result the UAW gained higher AIFs; COLAs were locked into immovable wage gains; and COLAs and AIFs were administered according to sliding scales. Labor and management compromised on three-year contract durations.

By 1961, auto companies began initiating contract alterations. GM asked for limits on COLAs, calling for "ceilings" to balance the "floors" on wage decreases, and for annual rather than quarterly COLA adjustments. (A 1960 steel industry settlement had included COLA ceilings.) In 1961, GM won neither request, but in 1967 achieved both. In 1970, wage ceilings ended and were never again reinstituted with workers recovering the wages they had been denied.

In spite of alterations, the company and the United Automobile Workers kept The Bargain longer than any others. Observing successfully stabilized labor relations, other companies initiated the principles of The Bargain: first, by halting the adoption of longer term contracts from 1948 to 1950; then, by greater use of escalation during the Korean War; and, by 1955, adding some form of productivity-based wages. Many industries that won longer-term contracts or escalator clauses provided a deferred wage increase in second, third or later years, but they did not call them "annual improvement factors," even though these often revolved around productivity considerations. Some bargainers provided long-term contracts with deferred increases but not escalation. More rarely, long-term contracts were adopted with escalation but without deferred increases.

Escalation Contracts Spread

Other unions besides automobile, automobile parts, farm implement industries and the electrical manufacturing workers received similar coverage. Meatpackers, a rare exception among food processors, used escalation, as did some construction, finance, insurance, real estate and service firms after 1966. Most major industries had longer-term contracts by 1959. Some even expanded upon the GM-UAW contract.

John Deere Company gave cost-of-living and annual-improvement-factor increases to all employees, including executives, for several years until company officials decided merit and performance raises were more effective in motivating employees. In 1955, General Electric workers negotiated a five-year contract and Teamsters made a six-year pact. Several years later, in 1974, unionized printers of the *New York Times* and the *New York Daily News* signed a ten-year pact which provided COLAs according to local prices, a 3-percent AIF and other benefits. Newspaper managers said the agreement helped to resolve longstanding resistance to automation.

Ceilings or "caps" on escalation were not prevalent until 1970, when they became part of 70 percent of all escalator clauses. That percentage declined to 25 by January of 1974. When companies instituted escalation ceilings, they often had floors and less-frequent adjustment and review of cost-of-living changes. There was movement from quarterly to semi-annual to annual reviews. During 1969-70, annual reviews applied to 75 percent of all escalated workers compared to 25 percent in 1966, with a return to 25 percent annual review coverage in 1974.

Escalation never covered more than fifty percent of workers in contracts involving one thousand or more workers, yet nonprotected workers felt its impact. For example, as much as steelworkers disliked UAW bargaining philosophies, their union used the GM-UAW contract as a departure point for straight wage increases.

As other important industries adopted the three concepts of The Bargain because of its successful stabilization of labor relations, others dropped it when more attractive benefits beckoned them. One million electrical equipment and railroad workers, troubled by the 1960 recession, dropped escalation in favor of supplementary unemployment benefits and reduced hours. A study of the overall ebb and flow of wage escalation indicated that when prices increased, escalation coverage rose, and when prices decreased, escalation dropped. Lags indicated that many waited for contracts to expire before they dropped escalation.

As they learned of worker protection from price increases, others sought the benefits of escalation. Australian lawyers introduced legislation which adjusted alimony to meet rising living costs. In Sweden, the first "cost-of-living" bonds were issued. A semi-public Swedish co-operative offered $19 million in twenty-year 3-percent bonds to be paid at maturity according to the cost of living. Bondholders would receive as much as $150 for every $100 invested, plus interest. An established floor would prevent any loss of invested money.

Some retirement benefits were protected from escalation. Under 1965 legislation, federal white collar employees and military personnel enjoy automatically adjusted annuities whenever the cost-of-living index increased 3 percent. A 1972 amendment to the Social Security Law automatically adjusted benefits. Federal food stamp participants received inflation protection in 1974. By 1975, 7.5 million union workers, 31.2 million Social Security recipients, 2.4 million retired federal employees, and 19.6 million food stamp users had escalation protection. Veterans Administration officials recently spoke about the possibility of indexing the GI Bill. Many landlords who lease office space, especially in northeastern cities since World War II, have written escalation clauses into their leases, based on percentage increases in operating costs to maintain their buildings. In 1976, Supreme Court justices even recognized the necessity of tying their salaries to living-cost increases. Millionaires Aristotle Onassis and Howard Hughes, recognizing the potential cost-of-living increases, protected their beneficiaries from inflation through escalated inheritance payments. Today, sixty million Americans have made their own Bargains.

Leading conservative economist Milton Friedman has recommended even more widespread applications of indexation particularly to translate fluctuating money values of payments into stable real value. University of Chicago economist and Nobel laureate Friedman urges Americans to "express all transactions that have a time duration in terms that eliminate the effect of inflation." He suggests that the government tie personal and corporate income taxes and government securities to the index. Friedman's economic views are applicable to every facet of government operation.

Tax brackets could be moved higher as inflation cuts into the purchasing power of increased incomes. To illustrate: a taxpayer in the $22,000-$26,000 bracket would pay 36 percent of his income in taxes. If indexation applied, and the cost of living increased 10 percent, that individual would need to earn between $24,200 and $28,600 to remain in the same 36 percent tax bracket. If he received a 6 percent income increase, then the individual would be in a lower tax bracket.

Under indexation of personal income taxes, the personal exemption, standard deduction and low-income allowance would be expressed as a given number of dollars multiplied by the ratio of the price index for that year to the price index for the base year selected. Capital gains consumed by increases in prices and decreases in the purchasing power of money would not be taxed. The base for calculating capital gains would be multiplied by the ratio of the price index in the year of sale to the price index in the year of purchase. The base for calculating depreciation on fixed capital assets would be adjusted in the same way.

For corporate taxation, capital gains and depreciation would be adjusted as would personal taxes. The dividing point between taxes and surtaxes would be in accordance with the price index increase or decrease. The cost of inventories used in sales would be adjusted to eliminate book profits or losses resulting from changes in prices between initial purchase and final sale.

Government securities would be adjusted to yield a maturity value equal to the face value multiplied by the ratio of the price index in the redemption year to the price index in the purchase year.

As government officials could issue these "purchasing power" securities, private firms could similarly offer long term bonds whose yields would likewise be adjusted for inflation, Friedman suggests. He further believes that company pension funds and savings and loan company loans should be indexed, adjusting both the assets supporting and the liabilities growing out of these economic tools.

In a reverse of the manner in which private sphere wage escalation spurred government application of indexation to some of its wages and welfare payments, government indexation might spur and support private indexation, predicts Friedman. For example, if income tax brackets rise as living costs rise, the added income an individual might earn from a corporate bond (if it were of the "purchasing power" type) would not be consumed by taxes, as it might if indexation had not been used.

Echoing Charles Erwin Wilson's words of thirty years ago, Friedman agrees that indexation is neither inflationary nor deflationary. Instead, Friedman sees it as a sop to the pains of withdrawing from inflation. The economist believes that widespread indexation would help create a more even reduction in inflation during times of Federal Reserve Board monetary restraint. Unemployment would rise less dramatically and disruptively and the lag between slowed total spending and a reduced inflation rate would be shorter.

If indexation becomes widespread, as Friedman suggests, The Bargain may prove to be the sale of the century.

7

The Bargain Picked Over

BEHIND CLOSED DOORS, the once angry young men of the thirties mellowed into middle-aged modifiers, ready to drop stubborn rancor for industrial statesmanship. The executives of General Motors borrowed an idea with previous radical and conservative associations, and made of it a middle ground from which both parties might move forward. One company, indispensable, with peace and prosperity for all—that promised to be a real Bargain. It was a steal. It stole from the UAW its wage abrasiveness and left it ready to work to their mutual benefit. It stole from the government an opportunity to gain more power from the impending crisis of inflation. And it stole into American life as a part of the "New Capitalism."

New

"New," The Bargain advertised itself, but this was not entirely true. There had been small-scale, temporary escalation attempts in a Sinclair Oil facility, at a Massachusetts shoe company and in a glass-making company in the U.S. Small-scale profit-sharing plans related to company productivity were tried previous to 1948, in Ohio electric and casting companies. But never before had the two concepts supported each other in this unique way, on so large a scale, with so impressive an impact. To almost all Americans, The Bargain was a totally new way of determining wages.

As never before, automobile workers anticipated annual wage increases, in spite of their authorization of wage *cuts* for the first time in history. Workers favored the annual improvement factor and minimized discontent over occasional cost-of-living wage decreases. United Auto Workers leaders encouraged members to sustain the contract and trust in management followed.

The agreement reversed patterns. "The UAW representatives usually approached GM first for wage contracts, and then went to others to establish principles," automotive reporter Tom Kleene said. In 1948, principles won acceptance because inflation seemed likely. In previous years, labor might have pressed harder for more money, but this time the union "sacrificed" wages for desirable principles.

General Motors pioneered for a change. Victor Reuther remembered that the UAW normally looked to Ford, and perhaps Chrysler, for innovations. Ford, a single-family firm, could more easily initiate new ideas because the opinions of Wall Street financiers did not complicate their decision making as in other companies. The strong leadership of Charles Erwin Wilson was evidenced as he convinced GM's board of directors and financial leaders of the viability of introducing wage escalation. In 1948, this influence contributed toward temporarily usurping the steel industry's usual role as the nation's heavy-industry wage pattern setter.

Normally, leaders of society use proven methods to maintain their lead. In this case, the largest industrial union and the richest company thrust themselves into an uncertain future with their experimental bargain. Why did they try something so innovative? Did they feel so secure in their own power? If so, little warranted it. Would-be kings and other enemies could still threaten Reuther's new power. The attempt on his life hinted of the dangers. Plants needed organizing. Finances required strengthening. Prosperity might dissipate worker discontent, which heightened union resolve. General Motors also had little reason to be smug. Only two years previously, the UAW deprived GM of four months of production, four months which other companies enjoyed. A reviving Ford Motor Company "stole" a GM executive to renew its own operations. Excessive security can not explain the willingness of GM and the UAW to try something new.

More than anything else, lively, unorthodox and timely leadership allowed The Bargain. Other industries could not summon such strong, forward-looking union and company presidents. Wilson and Reuther grasped their importance in postwar America. Both leaders looked far beyond isolated special interests to the complex larger sphere.

Wilson defended his broad economic theories, and convinced GM board members to cast aside misgivings. He assured them that the formula would rationalize operations and aid profit and production predictability. Productivity would pay wages, and the country would prosper from labor peace. His engineering principles, colored by his overwhelming sense of humanity, worked before in the Dayton Delco plant, where he had rehired employees displaced by consolidation of ignition work, saving the company $5 million yearly. Wilson and his bold ideas had a winning way. Both his practical and humane considerations helped inspire his ideas influenced by heartfelt reasoning.

Reuther overcame workers' previous fears of wage escalation, for he held that escalation made sense when combined with a productivity factor. He trained workers to respect longer-term contracts, and to anticipate new bargaining vistas. His power, enhanced by his expulsion of Communists from the unions and by the assassination attempt, stood behind his support of the 1948 contract.

The experiment was new to the parties and to most of the country. United Automobile Workers negotiators intially asked for twenty-five-cent hourly raises for workers to make up for increased living costs since June, 1946. They reminded General Motors that wages must improve purchasing power and reflect worker contributions to industrial efficiency. Seaton, midway in the negotiations, had commented that General Motors hoped to achieve more earnings for workers, more production for the company and a better living standard for everyone. The General Motors principles responded so directly to these proclamations that one wondered if negotiations had been rehearsed. Some United Automobile Workers bargainers believed the principles were counterproposals by Seaton and Anderson to their own documents and demands. Seaton and other General Motors men attested that they were Wilson's notions, developed long before 1948 and readied for this proper moment. Victor Reuther thought his brother raised demands without specifics, giving Wilson freedom of movement. He claimed, "Wilson had a very significant role in coming forward with a specific formula, but Walter conceived and dramatized the need and indicated that this was something that had to be dealt with through the collective bargaining mechanism."

Veteran labor reporter Jack Crellin conjectured the possibility that Wilson might have discussed the formula with Reuther prior to 1948. Wilson and Reuther respected each other and debated publicly. Civic meetings brought them together in situations where they might have had private discussions. On the other hand, the union leader might have inadvertently discovered the projected formula. General Motors board member Alfred P. Sloan, Jr. wrote National Industrial Conference Board president Virgil Jordan a detailed summary of Wilson's ideas, which might have been discussed in inner industrial circles. Information leaked about the General Motors proposal could easily have reached Reuther. The arguments Reuther's men presented during negotiations could have been bait for Wilson's proposals.

However possible, prior knowledge was improbable. If Wilson had in fact informed Reuther directly prior to 1948, GM's delay of the package almost until the strike deadline would not have had its intended effect. If Reuther had known, he most probably would have told his men to force the issue early so they could discuss specifics and work toward generous money terms. UAW executive board meeting minutes reveal that the principles presented by General Motors surprised UAW negotiators.

Improved

"Improved," The Bargain promised because it used tacit economic realities and statistical tools to promote labor peace. This would be a welcome improvement on arbitrary, "shotgun" bargaining based on a raw power struggle. The Bargain prompted inevitable wage increases while it eased expected strife. Cost of living pressure had often activated wage demands. In 1950, Wilson showed with detailed charts that, if adopted in 1910, the formula would have rendered average hourly wages within a few cents of existing wage rates, and the historical unrest and strikes would have been avoided. Workers had gained cost-of-living-adjusted raises equal to average national productivity. Previous to the 1948 contract, no short-term relationship between productivity and wage increases existed, and guesswork, rather than researched formulas, related previous living costs to wages. Because both parties accepted collective bargaining and government statistics to derive a basic formula, the approach lasted. If labor had not been involved in educating the worker economically, The Bargain would have been impossible. Since its 1937 victory and especially in the long 1946 strike, the UAW had been using statistics to remind the worker that his real wages had not kept up with living costs.

Noninflationary

The Bargain also promised to improve difficult

economic conditions, where high living costs lingered yet depression also threatened. Skeptics labelled the agreement inflationary, a claim that continues to be a point of contention.

Wilson, in his day, frequently responded to this charge. His most important reply was his "letter to Mr. X", dated August 24, 1951, and reprinted in many U.S. newspapers. In the letter, he repeated his argument that The Bargain would be neither inflationary nor deflationary, but would adjust wages *after* prices increased or decreased. Interestingly, Wilson agreed with the opinions of many union leaders and Communists in attesting that wages seldom pushed up prices. He suggested that cost-of-living adjustment might even *resist* inflation to some extent because of a slight lag between price changes and wage adjustment.

The company president stated that GM dividends created more inflation than COLAs did, because only $40 million went to workers compared with the $176 million to stockholders. One shareholder later wrote company officials: "If that is what he really believes, the shareholders of General Motors should get themselves another boy."

In 1948, alternatives seemed more inflationary than the proposed settlement. Inflation appeared certain, and a fixed wage scale looked vulnerable to discontent within months. Possible work stoppage threatened to curtail production and, in a high demand market, to raise prices.

At the same time, expedient solutions might not wear well, but Wilson looked beyond the convenient moment. He defended his principles as viable over time for the U.S. capitalistic economy. They were not inflationary wage principles because they *followed* cost-of-living changes and stayed within the balance productivity provided, he insisted. He even thought the country could bear the cost of higher wages, insurance policies and pension plans, because he believed that technological progress and worker productivity made increased compensation possible as well as desirable. Wilson thought that government tax, credit and budget-balancing policies especially caused inflation. Underlying his convictions about COLA and AIF was a strong sense that workers should be assured the purchasing power of their dollars and improved living standards so that mass industry would continue to have a healthy mass market for its products.

Little mention was made in 1949—even by Wilson—of that fact that General Motors, too, faced inflation—in its costs. These could not simply be absorbed by raising prices, for excessive prices might cut back the market. Comparing 1948 with the depression years, 1936-1941, GM officials noted that dividends on a per-share basis increased 30 percent; employment, 56 percent; and payrolls and dollar sales each went up to 180 percent. Clearly, the cost of living was increasing for automakers. Auto prices had increased slightly more than the average cost of living, but key items had increased more than autos in price, during this period. Further, autoworker wages increased more than both average living costs and prices of autos. Actually, more people had more money with which to buy more cars at higher prices, but it was uncertain just how long this state would last. In order to pay increased automaking costs, increased wages, increased capital expenses and still maintain a healthy profit margin, automakers needed a high level of efficient production plus suitable car prices to keep sales moving. The Bargain helped answer the former priority for GM. In its own way, it helped both the company and its workers cope with inflation.

In the thirty years since its inception, The Bargain appears to have fostered a labor peace that restrained inflation-whetting strikes and work stoppages. The contract may also have encouraged an "inflationary psychology", whereby protected workers, without any reason to change buying habits, fail to trigger automatic capitalistic mechanisms which normally adjust inflation.

The Bargain has neither caused nor cured inflation.

Rather it has tended to sustain worker purchasing power in the face of inflation caused by government deficit spending and money supply growth. These were inflationary factors Wilson anticipated. He did not predict the more recent inflation spurred by the 1974 OPEC quadrupling of oil prices. Escalated workers have been protected from this inflation, too.

Although many respected leaders argue that COLA and AIF cause inflation, there has been little proof to back their convictions. Studies tend to side with Wilson's conclusion that such wages follow inflation, and seldom contribute to it. Wilson remained alone with his "co-operation with inevitable wage increase" stand until studies inevitably co-operated with him.

Researcher Benson Soffer demonstrated that the GM-UAW formula sustained real wages during inflation, but shortchanged wage increases during stable price periods. He discovered that during inflation, escalated wages responded quickly to price movements. To keep apace the cost of living allowances, conventional contracts reopened often, so that wages rested on an implicit escalator basis when only a small number were explicitly covered. When nonescalated industries faced frequent wage reopenings, they projected excessive price increases into their wage settlements, often exceeding automatic increases. In such cases, cost of living allowances thwarted inflation, comparatively speaking. During stable price periods, automatic increases often failed to equal negotiated straight increases.

A Brookings Institution study assessed that the contract would create inflation if annual improvement factors spurred price increases or if the price index responded to wage stimulants outside the escalated sector. Originally Wilson formulated annual improvement factors as self-sufficient, paying their own way through increased productivity, and not requiring price increases. He also intended cost of living adjustments to pay for inflation caused by outside elements over which employees had little control.

Wages increased beyond Wilson's original limits, and outside factors spurred prices upward, yet studies still showed that the formula, over an extended period, did not create inflation. From 1946-69, the average real labor compensation, adjusted for Consumer Price Index changes including pensions, benefits and other additions, increased 2.7 percent hourly each year. This approximated the 2 to 3 percent average annual productivity increase which paid for all wage increases. A more recent government study showed that between 1966 and 1975, wage escalation did not create nor did little to sustain inflation. That same research warned that more frequent adjustments and smaller Consumer Price Index increments might make escalation inflationary.

The previous studies avoided judgments that The Bargain might hinder self-correction of economic imbalances resulting in more inflation. Escalation undermines the assumption that prices and wages will respond to unemployment and other restraints on demand. If both the employee and employer agree to protect themselves against national price advances, government action (tax increases) to decrease demand in the economy carries less weight.

Protected workers continue to buy. The natural brake inflation exerts on buying is eased. Albert Sindlinger Associates, a private research team, found that escalated workers expressed more regular optimism and spent more than they saved, especially when compared with stockholders. From another angle, high loan-interest rates and unemployment, which normally decrease prices, might fail to do so if companies remain committed to wage increases. Built-in economic balances are then disrupted.

The agreement arose during a postwar population and economic boom. Few contemporaries visualized how the formula would work under changed conditions. For example, National Planning Association economists recently predicted a shrinking birthrate and a curtailed gross national product by the turn of the century, and judged that annual productivity, which averaged three percent since World War II, might decline. A 3-percent annual improvement factor would become inflationary under such circumstances.

Generous

"Generously," The Bargain humbly offered. As reporter Jack Crellin said about General Motors, "They always claim to be generous whenever they give money away." Most settlements never completely satisfy labor leaders who traditionally win great victories; but the battle is never over for their "constituents," the workers. Among industrial peers, General Motors looked too generous, as it had disrupted a "no third-round wage increase" drive.

General Electric and the United States Steel companies turned down their worker requests for increases. Packinghouse workers struck, and won only a nine-cent hourly wage increase that the companies officially offered before the strike. The Ford Motor Company, the highest automobile wage payer, threatened to cut wages. Chrysler Corporation workers refused a six-cent offer, and were on strike at the time of the General Motors settlement.

Considering the industrial climate of the day, General Motors definitely was generous. Any raise over six cents per hour outdid automobile industry offers. Within the realm of possibilities, their profits allowed that General Motors was prudent not pennypinching. The company might have ignored formal principles and settled for implicit cost-of-living pay adjustments, as Virgil Jordan suggested. General Motors chose, instead, to grant workers formalized cost-of-living assurances as well as sure gains through annual improvement factors. Workers won what more often than not amounted to less delay between price or productivity increases and compensation under contracted formulas. It was a bargain for secure expectations, generous to the company as well as the workers in this respect. The UAW promised to give up the agonizing uncertainty of wrangling in deference to the clear-cut mechanism of the Bureau of Labor Statistics index and the General Motors–United Automobile Workers formula. The union vowed to honor technological progress without disruption, and to earn annual improvement increases in exchange.

Communists accused United Automobile Workers leaders of short-sighted stupidity. General Motors co-opted or compromised the union through The Bargain, they complained. Such complaints ring with political disaffection, understandable from a group recently evicted from union importance. The Communist press consistently countered enemy Reuther as much as big business during this period. Anything Reuther did received their opposition.

Communist criticism might have had some validity, had the United Automobile Workers lost strength in agreeing to The Bargain. The compromise integrated the union more into company operations but also bound the company more to the demands of the United Automobile Workers as a permanent, strong entity with its own purpose and process. General Motors could not usurp the union's role, and attempts to contain it within company-desired bounds met cunning resistance as often as compliance. General Motors needed a working force. While the United Automobile Workers held that fact in its grasp, it recognized that workers without employers lost their power. General Motors believed it bought labor peace with The Bargain; the UAW considered it a "springboard for progress."

The "benevolent" aspect of The Bargain is comparable to Henry Ford's famous five-dollar-a-day wage in 1914, since the General Motors offer was seen as both a means for the company to inspire worker loyalty and a method of assuring workers enough money to buy company products. In the Ford example, the wage brought workers into a more disciplined family company, with patriarch Henry Ford watching over the private lives of workers and rewarding them for good conduct. In 1948, GM and the UAW cooperated more fruitfully around better-understood rules of collective bargaining and broader economic statistics. Worker loyalty was directed more toward the economic system which developed collective bargaining and Bureau of Labor Statistics activity, rather than on a narrow corporate focus.

New. Improved. A generous bargain. These adjectives described many well-advertised packages in 1948, and this bargain was no exception. Yet in its day it was something more than a novel gimmick to try out on an unwitting public. It was the private sector's new deal for new times. Optimistically, a Good Deal in Good Times.

Longer Lasting

Like a wife, over the years, the Bargain disappointingly did not keep its shape but happily kept its vows for the most part. UAW members won skilled-worker inequity wages to offset the equalizing tendency resulting from using an average worker wage as a basis for annual improvement factors and cost of living allowances. Unskilled workers who gained greater-than-average proportionate increases from cost-of-living allowances and annual improvement factors equalizing tendencies never offered to return their "excesses" to company coffers. Later, as mentioned earlier, the parties agreed to stairstep the improvement increase according to predetermined wage categories to avoid inequities. In 1967, for example, the annual improvement factors ranged from nine through twenty cents per hour.

The productivity percentage, on which the annual improvement factor was tacitly based, got fatter—from 2 to 3 per cent. Meanwhile, the price index increase required to increase wages got thinner. The union kept its floor under wage cuts when prices fell. Management only temporarily had its ceiling on wage increases as prices soared. In some years, previous cost-of-living gains were transferred to permanent, untouchable wage increases.

Occasionally, cost of living allowances have been diverted to other designated purposes. Currently, 1 percent of General Motors' cost of living increase per quarter for six quarters will go towards lump sum payments to certain retirees and surviving spouses. The United Automobile Workers did not stop with cost-of-living allowances and annual improvement factors as Wilson had perhaps idealistically anticipated. The establishment of wages that kept up with living costs and allowed for improved living standards possibly freed union leaders to demand more fringe benefits: pensions, insurance policies and supplementary unemployment benefits, for example. Perhaps these demands would have been made just the same, with or without The Bargain. Nonetheless, it lived up to its promise of wages that met living costs and improved living standards. Even in the measurement of the cost of living by the Consumer Price Index, the standard of living improvement reflected the ever lower percentage of wages spent on subsistence goods, with an ever-increasing proportion going to luxury goods.

Prices increased; wages responded. This would have happened with or without wage escalation. Sometimes nonescalated workers won wages that exceeded wages gained automatically by escalated workers. Other times the opposite was true. Anticipation of inflation, not the existence of The Bargain, incited wage-increase demands in the past and always will in the future. The Bargain never promised to keep up with the nonescalated workers. It promised and did keep up with price increases in as systematic and as scientific a manner as possible. For both General Motors and the union, it successfully eliminated considerable guesswork, strikes and uncertainty.

The Bargain lived up to its promise of longer-lasting, more secure contracts because of its built-in dependency on the Consumer Price Index and because union leadership was more secure and committed. The first two-year pact was kept, which was an improvement upon previous yearly negotiations. In 1950, the overextended five-year term failed. It enabled union and management leaders to find their happy medium in three-year contracts, which became the stabilized, regular period of the contract.

Time Tested

The Bargain definitely lived up to its promise of labor peace. The contract prevented strikes and the inflationary shortages they cause, at least for General Motors and the United Automobile Workers. After 1948, few wage complaints spawned strikes. Fear of cost-of-living wage losses reopened the 1950 contract in 1953, and the removal of wage-escalation ceilings was an issue in the 1970 strike. Otherwise, only production standards and other non-economic local plant disputes occasioned subsequent conflict between General Motors and the United Automobile Workers. The company had lost about 130 million man hours in the 1945-46 strike but in the next ten years they lost only about forty million man hours because of work stoppages. Not until 1970 did a national strike rob the automobile company of as many man hours as the 1945-46 strike. General Motors' Louis Seaton, who has had a leading voice in General Motors labor relations from The Bargain's inception through the 1970's, credited the compact for industrial peace. Prosperity, which the agreement indirectly fostered, probably also prompted the harmony, as did more stable United Automobile Workers politics.

The productivity factor, as promised, eased technological dislocation. In 1948, union members dropped their former conviction that "machines take the bread out of workers' mouths," and formally agreed that to improve living standards, workers needed to accept technological progress, better tools, improved methods, new processes and modern equipment. They agreed that "to produce more with the same amount of effort is a sound economic and social objective." Wilson reminded UAW members frequently that strikes, work restrictions, featherbedding, absenteeism and artificially short work weeks might dissipate such progress. GM labor relations vice president George B. Morris, Jr. asserted that without AIFs the company could "have had trouble from those affected by the introduction of new techniques, or others fearful that their jobs, too, would be affected by future changes." Industries with the highest technological progress were the ones more likely to adopt productivity-related wage increases than others.

Time tested The Bargain. It passed, with such success that other industries looked to its lessons with great interest.

Time had also honored The Bargain, marking a crucial turning point. Never again would events, institutions, leaders and needs fit together in such a state waiting for ideas whose time had come. After The Bargain was signed, American labor and management entered a new era.

Was 1948 a fresh start, or just a breathing spell between wars and depressions? No one knew. All anyone could be sure of was that there was an inheritance of rules, new institutions and problems from past crises.

Depression years brought to 1948 the legacy of organized, recognized industrial unionism with collective bargaining rights. The Wagner Act of 1935 outlawed "company" unions and called for federally supervised worker elections to determine majority union representation. The law had legitimized trade unionism. Without it, Reuther would have had no solid group to lead and Wilson would not have prepared principles. Without the law, there would have probably been no forum equal to the task of taking years of statistics and turning them into a decision that would satisfy both parties so far into the future.

By 1948, the union became capable of educating the

worker about benefits of The Bargain and of assuring the contract's continuity during cost-of-living downturns. If government had imposed escalation from without, management might have feared it as an affront to the employer's privilege of determining wages with labor. If either government or management had imposed escalation on the worker from without, the worker's fears of status-quo wages and paternalism might have reared up.

The success during the depression of industrial trade unionism, an alternative to craft unionism, created circumstances favorable for The Bargain. At the 1935 AFL Convention, John L. Lewis tried to convince officials of the need to organize workers along industry-wide lines (coal, steel, auto, etc.) rather than in craft categories (electricians, bakers, bricklayers, etc.). Lewis created a Committee on Industrial Organization within the AFL. The committee was considered temporary, because AFL leaders wanted to divide prospective industrial union members among the existing craft unions. They suspended CIO members from the 1936 AFL Convention. The CIO members began to organize the unorganized and challenge AFL jurisdiction. Their success in the 1936 sit-down strike at GM won them much worker support, and by late 1937 the CIO was a permanent organization with more members than the AFL. In the late 1930's, employer and government reaction to union militance gave the more moderate AFL a temporary edge, and its membership began to surpass CIO membership.

That the automobile workers' representatives at the 1948 bargaining table were from CIO affiliates, not AFL unions was important to The Bargain. Craft unions have traditionally tried to limit their numbers, increase the demand for products, decrease the supply, and win higher wages. They also tended to decrease the amount of work each worker did, to decrease unemployment possibilities. Industrial union membership, by nature and philosophy, became more inclusive than exclusive. Their policy was to encourage more workers to produce more in order to eventually earn more. The Bargain's AIF, based tacitly on productivity, harmonized more with CIO than AFL philosophies.

War years brought to the 1948 bargaining table a legacy of labor-management teamwork. War also taught the postwar labor and business leaders, notably Wilson and Reuther, how their institutions influenced each other and the nation. War made the dedicated young Reuther visible to the equally vital Wilson. Wilson served on the labor-management committee assigned planning responsibility for the conversion of automobile plants to war production. Wilson's superior, William Knudsen, headed the Office of Production Management along with Sidney Hillman, with Walter Reuther as his special assistant. The debates during the war which Wilson and Reuther held in the GM Building on the topic of conversion were fair and friendly, a contrast to the atmosphere of the sit-down strike five years earlier. The debates set a precedent of mutual respect in public which resurfaced as the two joined in support of The Bargain and the subsequent agreements.

The war taught them both how much the automobile factories could produce when situations demanded it and when strikes did not disrupt production. It showed that labor organization, once an unknown danger to management, could be a positive force for efficiency within factories if its interests were respected and its membership and leadership secured. Wartime maintenance of membership clauses (once a worker joined a union, it was permanent) helped the UAW and other CIO unions which lacked the union shop or the closed-shop protection that many AFL unions had.

The immediate postwar days did not nullify the labor and management inheritances from depression and war, although there were rumors of reaction. Instead of going backwards to precrisis norms, both parties saw possibilities for moving forward on the strengths the crises had left in their wake. Employers bargained patiently instead of retaliating forcefully during postwar strikes. Labor was still fairly tight and a full market awaited. Union members worried about unemployment, lost overtime gains, lost union membership and recognition gains. They thought they had not kept up with living costs. The autoworkers' 113-day strike in 1946 won neither the catch-up wage workers sought nor the public's affection. Exposure of Communism and gangsterism in unions hurt the public image of unions. Management gained protection from unfair labor practices in the Taft-Hartley Act of 1947, balancing labor's protection from unfair management practices in the Wagner Act of 1935.

If the political climate grew to favor business, the economic climate favored compromise, for the companies needed workers in the clamoring market of the day, and the unions flexed a strong withholding muscle. If the business world now had more public and political sympathy, it could still not risk old tactics of labor spies, strikebreaking and such to regain lost power. Management needed to work with the union, to satisfy mutual needs, yet it needed to define its terms and limits, too.

Charles E. Wilson especially took the chance. Instead of looking a short distance ahead to preventing further labor gains, as many executives did, he reached further for the perpetuation of labor peace. Reuther and the UAW accepted Wilson's gesture, because it responded to labor's legitimate needs, of which Reuther had made Wilson aware. Too, Reuther's power was more stable than ever. The Bargain made it possible for Reuther to develop a favorable public image, build his union, recover from the shooting, and avoid the bad publicity of an "inflation-causing" (as the public would claim) strike.

And so the pieces fit in 1948. Government inertia made room for private initiatives. Progressive leaders— adversaries of the friendliest kind—took forward steps. Strong private institutions stood ready to gain from cooperation. Ideas that suited the needs and philosophies of both parties were presented. Compromises worked because each compromiser felt compensated.

The giants of labor and industry signed The Bargain and the country was soon in the grasp of a new era in labor relations. What the sit-down strikes had been to labor strife and recognition, The Bargain would be to labor peace and anonymity.

Scientifically Formulated

Unlike any previous major settlements in United States history, this agreement stressed reliance on research and statistics. Cold, hard government data, more than hotheaded union officials battling hardhearted company officials, determined wages. It drained collective bargaining of drama and conflict, and made it more an educational debate among economists. It also robbed labor-management conflicts of their spectacular publicity. Photos of workers taking over factories and being beaten by hired thugs could capture a quicker, wider audience than graphs of the relationship between wages and prices. Bargaining went from public to private, from showmanship to sophistication.

If worker representatives "had exchanged their brickbats for briefcases," as reporter Tom Kleene described it at the time, it also became difficult to distinguish the labor from the business leader, in style and approach. The labor leader became more integrated, less alienated, more a natural working part of the system, more interested in making the system work than discarding it and starting anew like the worker he represented.

There was more structure and less political play within the union and between union and management. Whether Reuther survived politically because The Bargain channeled discontent over wages into a neutral mechanism, or whether The Bargain was possible because Reuther could enforce it in his union, is a "which came first" dilemma. It appears that the leader and the contract reinforced each other over time.

It was the right moment for workers to escape public

scrutiny, yet keep their power growing and their gains secure beneath the surface, which is what the contract allowed. The late forties and early fifties saw a reaction to Communism, bred by Cold War, and as far as unions were identified with Communism, they, too, were suspect.

As the UAW spurned Communists, it moved distinctly away from any possible concept of the workers as a class, separate from any other in substance or in goals. It did not want to rule as a class, only influence as an institution. This historic pact and the fringe benefits in its wake gave many workers the income and the benefits of a middle-class white-collar worker. The UAW fostered worker pride and unified strength; but the worker was a vital cog in the great American production machine worthy of his large, fair share through collective bargaining. This view was reaffirmed and extended.

The Bargain, with its systematic, peaceful approach to wage adjustment, countered the revolutionary fervor of Communists, who considered it company co-option of workers, in spite of Trotsky's earlier recommendations. Workers accepted wage escalation, contrary to Virgil Jordan's expectations, not waiting until they dominated national politics.

After the agreement, unions appeared more and more to be huge establishments on equal footing with management and government. Union leaders did not seem bent upon overthrowing government or taking over companies as they might have in the sit-down period. The UAW was now more sure of its sphere and its power after 1948. Collective bargaining gave them a channel for winning. If they could battle well across the table, why go elsewhere? Let companies and government play their roles, for unions were unprepared, nor did they want to direct the whole thing. The Bargain pointed the way and headed the union and management in the proper direction: each institution served its interests best by keeping a harmony of interests within divergent but overlapping spheres.

The quiet revolution of The Bargain channeled worker

wrath into statistics; the union began to foster a sense of belonging in place of belligerence. The worker belonged to the union as he belonged to a church, political party, or company. He was not a worker looking for a revolution because he already had an outlet for his discontent that was heeded. The Bargain had proved him worthy of upward mobility. What's more, he won pensions, life insurance, unemployment compensation, and membership in stock and savings programs. He became middle class in substance and mentality. Instead of feeling "exploited," victimized and deprived as he often did in the depression, the worker now saw himself benefitting from the prosperity he helped to create. His union helped; productivity and labor peace contributed. He was even being told that corporations gave him a privileged status. Although he contributed only partially to annual productivity, he gained from the total effort year after year.

The Bargain reaffirmed the private relationship between labor and management. The two agreed to use the government price index on their own terms. Before, the government had teamed with labor in what proved a shaky alliance—administrations changed, and even within administrations, leaders wavered, as John L. Lewis discovered with President Roosevelt. Because unions got perpetuated wage increases and the open door to further gains through The Bargain, they turned less and less to political channels for their demands. Unions grew more manageable for companies, and production more predictable, and so the relationship reinforced itself on both sides.

Together, labor and management insisted that worker wage increases do not cause inflation, but that government excesses and policies did. The Bargain promised to protect the worker from this inflation he did not cause. The corporation, in turn, could blame government for inflation in a peacetime economy because the worker, more than the government, would buy the products the company sought to produce in great quantities.

The worker had turned away from alienation towards

integration, towards more productivity and less disruption to reap the benefits of the system. The workers turned down the Communist approach.

This contract amounted to a great change for capitalism. New methods of competition, roles for government and systems of corporate organization already had reshaped the system in the twentieth century. Any more devices had to assure prosperity to survive. Most Americans, numbed by large institutions and economic forces, let private leaders covertly revise capitalism as long as their living standards improved. Workers empowered unions, and labor-management agreements empowered government statistics to deal with mysterious, sometimes overwhelming economic forces. Few complained.

The agreement highlighted collective effort. By nature, it would be more difficult for individuals to establish escalator-clause contracts for themselves under a boss or agency. Collective bodies more often brought real wage protection about through representatives. It would be more difficult for individuals, rather than representatives of corporations, unions or government programs to wield power on Bureau of Labor Statistics research advisory councils which determined how to render the Consumer Price Index.

The Bargain also helped the largest company and union survive and become larger. GM enforced union permanence, and the union won anticipated gains. The gains spurred Wilson to joke that the UAW now assumed it had to come up with its "new model" every year, just as the industry did. Wage questions lost the aura of conflict that attracted reporters and new union members, and the United Automobile Workers initiated new issues to replace wages. After 1948, the United Automobile Workers solidified its membership, organized more members and strengthened its finances. They tackled everyday shop problems, local seniority and wage questions and production standard grievances. By 1950, GM conceded a modified union shop which gave the UAW more security and prestige. Improved pension, insurance and vacation plans and special skill wage increases furthered UAW power with its members.

The United Automobile Workers then began to challenge Teamster Union political power in Michigan and in the nation. Through the years, United Automobile Workers has been able to turn to questions of job security, boredom on the assembly line and civil rights.

The company held onto its coveted managerial responsibilities: the right to hire, fire and transfer workers according to merit rather than seniority; to make technological changes; and to set prices and keep the company books private. The union sidetracked the "ability to pay" questions as GM made record profits. The company could now expand its multinational operations, consider the latest forms of scientific management and cope better with possible product competition from new entrants, foreigners or conglomerates with labor relations stabilized.

The settlement diminished the labor-management adversity which vitalized and balanced capitalism through countervailing powers. *Fortune* magazine noted Wilson's widely publicized letter explaining the contract: "Except for one or two sentences, the missive could easily have been composed in the United Automobile Workers research department at bargaining time." Ironically, another commentator saw the letter as a near duplicate of a Socialist Labor Party newspaper article, which considered existing unions to be working class enemies.

When unions and managements agreed more, the class struggle necessary to a Communist revolution naturally waned. Historian Frederick Lewis Allen noted that by sharing productivity throughout the economic pyramid, the U.S. avoided hard class stratification, escaped plutocracy and its response, Communism.

The UAW and GM co-operated for mutual strength, to regain dominion over private enterprise and sidestep excessive government influence. Harry S Truman, in his memoirs, admitted that long before he became president, he decided the country needed a national wage policy, effective mediation machinery and other remedial legislation. Government intervention was just as possible as government inertia. GM officials felt more immune from government intervention than steel and railroad companies, yet government fact-finding committees still intruded upon them.

Labor reporter Jack Crellin considered both GM and the UAW weak right after the war because "they had gone through a long period with the War Labor Board. . . in 1945-46, they were still constantly running to Washington." As negotiations approached, inflation remained troublesome in America, and neither GM nor the UAW wanted peacetime government wage-price determination. At the outset of the 1948 negotiations, UAW bargainer Art Johnstone bade General Motors men to soothe labor relations so that government would not feel compelled to interfere.

John Maynard Keynes's popular economic philosophy had stressed government responsibility to use fiscal tools to maintain economic stability and employment. As prosperity became a political responsibility, businessmen lost voice and status in economic affairs. The Bargain openly announced to the country that a company and a union would make up for government policy errors which caused inflation. They would protect workers from forces over which they felt they had little control. Balance between productivity and wage increases would provide stability and prevent inflation.

Postwar Americans needed hasty solutions. Unions seemed to compete among each other with "pie in the sky" wage demands, and this puzzled businesses because strikes in almost every major industry reaped settlements within one-half a cent of one another. Labor rankled over widespread layoffs and the loss of war overtime pay. Both parties worried that recovery programs and an increased military budget would push up car prices and aggravate inflation. Government added to their confusion with its unsure steps about wage and price controls. Stability intervened when the private sector used The Bargain and reasserted its initiatives in fostering labor peace, prosperity and economic stability.

Through industrial peace, GM and the UAW probably thwarted considerable government strike intervention, and the federal government followed the GM-UAW lead in its Korean War program. In spite of this seeming reassertion of private leadership, The Bargain ironically revealed the federal government's importance to both labor and management. The BLS index became the most important single government statistic. GM industrial engineers studied whether or not indirect government control might influence escalation, because government buying affected demand, and in turn, cost-of-living changes. The contract extended to workers what parity gave to farmers—income security according to government-administered statistics. Economists questioned whether the farmer, needing more money to buy machinery, might raise food prices, which would increase workers' living costs and therefore wages, and up the prices of machinery they made, and so on. No one dared strike out at farmers or workers, however, as long as they were in the hands of the unquestionable, objective government statistics. The farmer-worker support might combine to create an inflationary pattern off limits to criticism.

BLS operations hedged upon the privacy of both sides. Commissioner Ewan Clague said of his agency researchers, "We are right down in the streets, in your plants, in your stores and in your homes. We are statisticians in work clothes, both blue collar and white collar. . ." Sometimes labor or business representatives on research advisory councils appealed to the Secretary of Labor or Budget Bureau to overrule the BLS on a point of contention, but Clague said neither party tried to suppress or restrict agency work. The private sector grew more dependent than ever upon the "objective referee" the BLS provided.

The housewife wheeling her shopping cart now ultimately influenced the family's wages through her buying habits as much as her husband on the automobile assembly line through his productivity. "New capitalism" adjusted to a novel form of wage determination that looked away from company and local conditions to national economic statistics.

The Bargain usurped supply and demand bases for wages which John L. Lewis reviled in 1936, when he accused GM and the Ford Motor Company of dealing with labor "ruthlessly, as a commodity or an article of commerce. . . according to the law of supply and demand without regard to human standards of living."

As expected, strikes, strike threats or government intervention subsided as wage-determination pressures. The agreement also quelled Reuther's "ability to pay" arguments, strongly publicized since 1945-46. Negotiators talked less of prices and profits in subsequent negotiations, and gave GM management more of a sense of fixed authority.

The bargain has its historical place as an adaptive mechanism of new capitalism. It also speaks of corporate social conscience development and its relation to American social reform. The formula reached out to meet the workers' needs while it helped improve business. Gone were the days when businesses stressed the worker as an inhuman unit of production. Years of disruptive strikes and agonizing negotiations made management more attentive to worker needs. The new GM president even before 1948 had proved himself a man who *could* be bothered. To underscore job pride coincident with technological progress in the Delco-Remy plant, he had new equipment moved to the center of the factory floor, walls painted, equipment shined, glass partitions built around it and workers freshly uniformed. Reporters called the GM president at his home any time of the day or night. In the GM cafeteria, he often discussed work problems with secretaries and white collar workers. UAW leaders invited him to appear before their usually closed national General Motors council meeting with some time prior to 1948. He was the only corporate president Jack Livingston could recall who ever received that honor.

In 1941, at the time he became president of General Motors, Wilson was particularly concerned about labor relations. Nothing indicates that Walter Reuther spurred him to consider worker living costs and standards of living at that time. Reuther had not yet attained full power within the union, but Wilson must have been self-motivated to study such questions. Certainly he saw benefits to company profits and production if the project was well developed. However, he needed to consider what would satisfy workers, and at the same time, win their approval at the bargaining table. A plan which the UAW might reject would foment more distrust and dissension than ever. He looked for a way to ease labor fears of wage freezes from living-cost wage adjustment. He also needed to convince board members that Virgil Jordan's doubts about the wage escalation were unfounded. To allay these fears he developed the annual improvement factor.

What personally compelled Wilson in 1941 to explore innovative possibilities? Perhaps he needed to prove his competence to himself and his peers in those first days of his company presidency while he was briefly and unexpectedly hospitalized. Maybe he needed to assuage guilt over his wealth, like a latter-day Andrew Carnegie, so he looked for a project that would associate him with benevolence. Possibly, his devotion to the system which worked well for him, and under which he worked so well, emitted schemes to renew capitalism in changed conditions. Most likely, his practical, engineering mind, which always helped him improve his surroundings, combined with his natural humaneness to elicit the proposal. He was in a better position of power than ever to bring up new ideas.

Current myth presupposes that companies must be forced into adopting socially beneficial ideas that necessarily conflict with their profit making. Charles E. Wilson, along with UAW men, shattered this thinking when they co-operated in a type of socioeconomic reform little recognized before in our history.

The Bargain reformed capitalism, with the survival and well-being of its participants in mind. It reformulated wage policy through scientific principles and avoided leftist extremes through moderate changes. Moral motives and justification backed the policy. Wilson openly supported the premise that workers who did not create inflation should not suffer from it unnecessarily. The company president was a pioneer in attributing moral responsibility to management when he stated that companies which cannot meet average national productivity-improvement wage increases were incompetent.

The moral and practical motives of two natural opponents, Reuther and Wilson, combined in a mutual agreement to remedy some of the flaws of capitalism. The government became a responsible third party. Much typical American change and reform was attained in this case through collective bargaining rather than through the political mechanism.

Prevailing "liberal" framework of American reform pits the benevolent representative of the underdog against the powerful and corrupt establishment. The underdog tames his master, who loses power in the battle benefitting the masses. Other historians invert this theme to claim that the master only manipulated the underdog's representatives to achieve his own selfish ends, over time helping himself and appeasing public discontent. Intellectuals characterized antitrust and other reform legislation of the early twentieth century under both categories of thought.

The Bargain was ignored as social reform because it did not fit these preconceived notions and because the conflict in which it developed escaped public scrutiny. It evinced little public response until it became policy. Normally reform progressed from local to state to national government spheres. In this case, it moved from foreign applications and a few small operations (in its incomplete form) to the largest manufacturing company in the United States to other industries and government programs, eventually to even broader applications nationwide.

Unlike traditional social reform, it originated among the "haves," with the support of the "have nots." The idea that a business leader could mold and present reform to benefit company, worker and the public alike defied usual business practices and developed attitudes of suspicion even though it sustained and altered capitalism. That the private sector rather than government initiated it made it even more suspect. Let government institute massive aid to federal education, and it is part of our great reform tradition. On the other hand, let Andrew Carnegie dot the country with his libraries, and it is charity reaped from dubious business practices. The judgment follows that government acts but in the public interest, while business acts totally in a selfish, profit-oriented manner.

In Wilson's case, he knew the country needed a nongovernmental answer to inflation, and he devised a policy for General Motors suited to his business and to labor, too. Because he believed so strongly that the public would gain also, he crusaded in behalf of his principles to community and business groups across the nation. Conceivably, if business had acted solely in its own interest, legislation would have been enacted to enforce contracts of longer duration.

If the package had been applied nationwide, as Wilson envisioned, escalation would have elevated consumer interest. A person protected by escalation could continue to buy what he bought last year, in spite of economic conditions. He would be protected from inflation created by government, labor and business. He would even be protected from the price increases his own excessive demand created. Wilson assumed most industries would eventually adopt some form of his proposal. Any company able to survive the struggle of business life could pay wages along the lines the principles offered, he sincerely believed. Nonprotected workers might be hurt until they won wages which compensated for the lack of automatic adjustments or which exceeded escalated wage increases.

The Bargain proved that a practical social conscience might germinate within the private sphere, make policies intended to benefit wide constituencies and allay government impositions from without. Resultant labor peace helped the majority while the principles protected recipients from inflation.

Former bitter enemies reaped conciliation that spring day in 1948, and tilled mutual strength that proved private leadership could equal public initiative in reshaping capitalism. The question so often asked of government programs must be asked of this labor-management agreement: did this device of new capitalism contribute to the distinction of capitalism? Collective forces prevailed. A government agency became a permanent business-labor partner. A new form of wage determination stifled another element of Adam Smith's original dream. Yet the powers behind the contract—Reuther, Wilson and their organizations—professed highest devotion to the system.

Slight changes in capitalism probably seemed irrelevant in view of benefits involved. If collective forces gained, at least most of the countervailing powers grew together and could still offset each other. Labor, business, government and consumer all won something. If a government agency earned a permanent role, business and labor created and influenced that role which could still rescind it at a moment's notice.

The new wage determination only formulated a historical pattern. UAW and GM officials took a calculated risk with this device of new capitalism because each saw it as a means to prosperity immune from inflation. GM foresaw good profits from a high demand, high production economy amidst labor peace. The company overcame Virgil Jordan's warnings that escalation would prompt extensive government wage-price control. The UAW relished the thought that workers became more free from the vicissitudes of labor market competition. The union overruled previous fears of cost-of-living wage freezes, ignored (and perhaps welcomed) Communist critics, and looked forward to winning higher pay from the principles of the pact. The worker failed to achieve the dominance Communism promised him, but he did win the desirable goal of more security and progress within the capitalistic system.

In 1948, promises outweighed portents. The Bargain recalled previous implicit patterns of wage determination and emerged from within rather than being imposed from without. It was reversible, adaptable and could be used by any industry in the nation.

Probably both leaders sensed that widespread effects of The Bargain would appear only after the principles were widely instituted. American economy was too complex to easily analyze the impact of one untried device on it prior to adoption, and no one would know if capitalism thereby destroyed itself until some crisis allowed the new contract to be tested.

No crises arose. Both business and labor maintained close association influence on BLS advisory councils, and the overall BLS operation continued to satisfy them. They settled differences without government intervention. Business found other methods to compensate and curtail prices when lower consumer purchasing power indicated price and wage cuts. Predetermined wage increases prevented the latter and government only briefly enforced peacetime wage-price control.

When democracy and capitalism seemed to fall short of Americans' expectations, citizens criticized and worked to correct. A subtle revolution in capitalism followed. The Bargain was part of this process. It proved the economic system flexible enough to reconsider the needs of employers, employees and the public, and make adjustments. The Bargain tended to rescue capitalism's high drawing card—the high living standard—from inflation's ravages. It allowed prosperity, but made room for progress. The BLS index was dressed in the newer and finer garb of improved products and higher living standards every ten years or so, as the worker climbed his escalator upward. Some executives, white collar workers, government retirees, Social Security beneficiaries and food stamp recipients climbed aboard. Professors and Supreme Court justices sought to join them.

The Bargain marked a quiet, bloodless, formularized revolution of rising expectations. It would help make the country safe for capitalism.

Index